US SUPREME COURT LANDMARK CASES

ESTABLISHING THE RIGHTS OF THE ACCUSED
Miranda v. Arizona

DON RAUF and GAIL BLASSER RILEY

Enslow Publishing
101 W. 23rd Street
Suite 240
New York, NY 10011
USA
enslow.com

Published in 2017 by Enslow Publishing, LLC.
101 W. 23rd Street, Suite 240, New York, NY 10011

Library of Congress Cataloging-in-Publication Data

Names: Rauf, Don, author. | Riley, Gail Blasser, author.
Title: Establishing the rights of the accused : Miranda v. Arizona / Don Rauf and Gail Blasser Riley.
Description: New York, NY : Enslow Publishing, 2017. | Series: US Supreme Court landmark cases |
Includes bibliographical references and index.
Identifiers: LCCN 2016023944 | ISBN 9780766084285 (library bound)
Subjects: LCSH: Miranda, Ernesto—Trials, litigation, etc. | Trials (Rape)—Arizona. | Self-
incrimination—United States. | Right to counsel—United States. | Police questioning—United States.
Classification: LCC KF224.M54 R38 2016 | DDC 345.73/056—dc23 LC record available at
https://lccn.loc.gov/2016023944   17/02

Printed in Malaysia

To Our Readers: We have done our best to make sure all websites in this book were active and
appropriate when we went to press. However, the author and the publisher have no control over and
assume no liability for the material available on those websites or on any websites they may link to.
Any comments or suggestions can be sent by e-mail to customerservice@enslow.com.

Portions of this book originally appeared in the book *Miranda v. Arizona: Rights of the Accused.*

Contents

CHAPTER 1. Rights for the Accused 5

CHAPTER 2. History Leading Up to the Landmark Case 13

CHAPTER 3. Making a Case for Miranda 35

CHAPTER 4. Arizona's Argument Against Miranda 49

CHAPTER 5. The Supreme Court Rules 63

CHAPTER 6. The Legacy of Miranda 83

Questions to Consider 99

Primary Source Documents 103

Chronology 107

Chapter Notes 110

Glossary 119

Further Reading 123

Index 125

Acknowledgments

The author would like to offer special thanks to:

James M. Riley, Jr., Esq., for extensive assistance and legal expertise in preparation of this mansuscript.
Babs Bell Hajdusiewicz for tireless aid, friendship, and levity in preparation of this manuscript.
Kristine C. Woldy, Esq., for friendship, candor, and legal expertise in preparation of this manuscript.
Laurie Lazzaro Knowlton for insisting on "this whole writing thing."
Sally Lee, for getting the ball rolling on this book.
Peter Baird, Esq., for information and inspiration.
Moise Berger, Esq., for personally taking me back to the second Ernesto Miranda trial.
David Hoober and Carolyn Grote, and the staff of the Arizona State Archives, for everlasting assistance and consideration.
Ray Tevis and staff, Arizona Department of Library, Archives and Public Records.
Bill Shover and Nancy Van Leeuwen, *Arizona Republic*.
Franz Jantzen, Supreme Court Curator's Office.
Barbara Natanson and George Hobart, Library of Congress, Prints and Photographs Division.
Bebe Overmiller, Mary Eisen, and staff, Library of Congress, Photo Duplication Division.
Chris MacGregor and staff, Imagination Plus, The Woodlands, Texas.
Mark Meader and staff, National Archives, Motion Picture Sound and Video Branch.
John Vandereet, National Archives, Civil Division.
Kathleen Schrader and staff, Phoenix, Arizona Police Department Records Division.
Melissa Thompson, Maricopa County Attorney's Office.

— Gail Blasser Riley

CHAPTER 1

Rights for the Accused

You have the right to remain silent. Anything you say can and will be used against you in a court of law. You have the right to talk to a lawyer and have him present with you while you are being questioned. If you cannot afford to hire a lawyer, one will be appointed to represent you before any questioning, if you wish one.

Many Americans are familiar with these words from TV crime shows and movies. The statement is known as the "Miranda warning" or "Miranda rights." Police in the US give the warning to criminal suspects who are in custody and going to be interrogated (formally questioned about a crime). These words are designed to make the accused aware of their rights. Law enforcers must read a suspect his rights to assure that a person's statements can be used as evidence against him or her in a court of law. Since the Miranda rights were established by the Supreme Court in 1966, people have argued their pros and cons. Many say these rights help provide justice and fairness for the accused, while others have said they have made it more difficult to get a confession from those who are genuinely guilty of a crime. While the Miranda warning has undergone decades of interpretation since being introduced, it is still a criminal procedure rule that law enforcers must follow. And it all started with the case of kidnapping and rape on March 2, 1963.

Here a police officer is reading someone the Miranda warning from a printed card.

A Violent Crime in Arizona

The theater screen had been anything but silent on this night. Guns had blazed, and dying men had screamed. But *The Longest Day* had come to an end. Credits had rolled, and the movie theater in Phoenix, Arizona, was quiet again.

Eighteen-year-old Rebecca Ann Johnson (in courtesy to the victim, her real name is not used) finished her duties at the theater refreshment counter and took a few minutes to visit with a fellow worker. It was 11:30 p.m. when, as usual, Rebecca Ann left the Paramount Theater to head for the bus stop.[1]

She could not have known, however, as she boarded the bus, that her nightly routine was about to be shattered. On that March night in 1963, the life of Rebecca Ann Johnson would, in a matter of hours, be changed forever. She was on the verge of being drawn into one of the most controversial landmark cases in the history of the United States Supreme Court.

It was 12:10 in the dark morning hours when Rebecca Ann stepped off the bus and began her short walk home. As she walked, a light-green car pulled sharply out of a driveway. Rebecca Ann jumped back to avoid being hit. The car pulled into the street, moved a short distance, and stopped.

Rebecca Ann was caught unaware when a man from the car approached and grabbed her around the waist. The assailant covered her mouth and warned, "Don't scream, and I won't hurt you."[2]

On March 3, 1963, Ernesto Miranda kidnapped the terrified Rebecca Ann Johnson. He forced her to lie down in the back seat of his car, bound her hands and feet with rope, and then drove to the Arizona desert, where he raped her. Afterward, he asked her to give him her money. She handed over the four dollar bills she had on her.

Approximately two hours after he had grabbed her from a Phoenix street, Miranda returned Rebecca Ann to her neighborhood. Oddly, his parting words were: "Whether you tell your mother what has happened is none of my business, but pray for me."

Rebecca Ann ran from the car, too frightened to check the license plate number. She raced the few blocks home and, between sobs, spilled the details to her sister.[3]

The man who was eventually found guilty of committing the horrifying crime against her was Ernesto Miranda. His name was to become a verb in the English language as police, prosecutors, defense attorneys, and judges would speak of "Mirandizing" a suspect for decades to come.

The Police Investigation

Rebecca Ann detailed her terrifying night to police. She described her attacker and his automobile. Specifically, she told police that a long rope had been draped across the back of the front seat, perhaps for passengers to pull up on to get out of the car.[4] The rope was not used for the crime but was a distinct feature in the assailant's vehicle. It was clue that could help lead to the criminal's capture.

During repeated interviews, Rebecca Ann's detailed statements were sometimes inconsistent. She was said to be

Rebecca Ann Johnson's description of the unique features of Ernesto Miranda's car played a large part in helping the police find and arrest him.

slightly mentally challenged so this may have affected her account of the crime. Her description of the route to and from the desert posed inaccuracies. Further problems arose when Rebecca Ann was subjected to a polygraph test, or lie detector test. Officers began to doubt whether Rebecca Ann was telling the truth.[5]

On March 9, 1963, at approximately 11:45 p.m., Rebecca Ann's brother-in-law was on his way to meet her at the bus stop. He saw a car matching her description of the attacker's automobile. It had a light-green color and brown upholstery. He noted the license plate number, and reported it to the police.

Miranda is shown here in his booking photos. Because of his case, police are required to inform suspects of their rights upon arrest.

Detectives ran a check and found an almost identical license number. They traced the number to an address where they found the matching license plate on a Packard automobile parked in the driveway. Inside the car, officers spotted a rope draped across the back of the front seat. Ernesto Arturo Miranda was taken into custody.

At the police station on that same day, March 13, 1963, Rebecca Ann thought she recognized Miranda in a lineup. But she wasn't positive.

After the lineup, police took Miranda to an interrogation room, a room for questioning.

"How did I do?" Miranda asked.

"You flunked," answered one of the officers.[6]

This response was not accurate, as Rebecca Ann had not been able to make a positive identification. Nonetheless, the detectives

CITY OF PHOENIX, ARIZONA
POLICE DEPARTMENT

SUBJECT: RAPE   DR. 63-08380

STATEMENT OF: ERNEST ARTHER MIRANDA

TAKEN BY: C. Cooley #413 - W. Young #182

DATE: 3-13-63   TIME: 1 30/ Pm PLACE TAKEN: Interr Rm #2

I, Ernest A. Miranda, do hereby swear that I make this statement voluntarily and of my own free will, with no threats, coercion, or promises of immunity, and with full knowledge of my legal rights, understanding any statement I make may be used against me.

I, Ernest A. Miranda, am 23 years of age and have completed the 8th grade in school.

EAM — Seen a girl walking up street stopped a little ahead of her got out of car walked towards her grabbed her by the arm and asked to get in the car. Got in car without force tied hands + ankles. Drove away for a few miles. Stopped asked to take clothes off. Did not, asked me to take her back home. I started to take clothes off her without any force, and with cooperation. Asked her to lay down and she did. Could not get penis into vagina got about ½ (half) inch in. Told her to put clothes back on. Drove her home. I couldn't say I was sorry for what I had done. but asked her to say a prayer for me. EAM.

I have read and understand the foregoing statement and hereby swear to its truthfulness.

WITNESS: _____ Ernest A. Miranda
Wilfred M. Young #182

Miranda signed this confession on March 13, 1963. Though it states his rights at the top, the argument was that he had not been made aware of them at the time of his arrest.

began questioning Miranda, and he signed a confession approximately two hours later.

What would happen to Miranda's confession in court? Would he later deny his confession? Would Rebecca Ann Johnson be able to identify her attacker at the trial? How would a surprise witness help win a conviction? Why, out of thousands of kidnappings and rapes that had come before, would Ernesto Miranda's case be decided by the Supreme Court and affect every arrest in the United States from that day forward?

CHAPTER 2

History Leading Up to the Landmark Case

T hroughout history, governments have often treated those accused of crime unfairly. For example, some have allowed the use of torture to get a confession. When the accused can be judged unfairly, it may lead to the rise of tyranny and individuals may lose their rights. When the colonists in America were forming the basis for a new government in the United States, they were wary of tyranny and unlimited government. Although the people of Britain were relatively free compared to other countries, American colonists felt they had suffered legal abuses. They wanted a government that would help protect people from being punished for crimes they did not commit and from being convicted in unfair trials. To achieve this, the creators of the Constitution and the Bill of Rights included a series of protections for individuals accused of committing crimes in America. The *Miranda* ruling, hundreds of years later, was another measure in a long line of decisions designed to help protect a suspect's rights, even if that suspect turned out to be guilty in the end.

The Right Against Self-Incrimination

One of the rights being addressed in Miranda's case has to do with protecting against incriminating yourself. The US government forbids compelling any person to give testimonial evidence that would likely incriminate him or her during a criminal case. This right is protected by the Fifth Amendment to the Constitution, which was ratified in 1791. (It is part of the Bill of Rights, which are the first ten amendments that became part of the Constitution that year.) The Fifth Amendment states: "No person ... shall be compelled in any criminal case to be a witness against himself ... "

A defendant may choose to testify, give information on the witness stand about a case, or may choose not to testify. Failure to testify may not be used against the defendant, nor may it be considered for any purpose. Indeed, if the defendant does not testify, the prosecutor, the lawyer representing the state, and the victim may not even mention the defendant's failure to testify to the jury.

The roots of this law go back the seventeenth-century trial of John Lilburne in England. John Lilburne, a Puritan publisher, was charged with the crime of bringing books into England that incited people to rebel against the authority of the monarch. At the time, the Church of England was opposed to Puritanism.

When ordered to the Star Chamber (an English court of law which was known for its forceful interrogation), Lilburne steadfastly refused "'to take a legal oath' and 'answer truly.'" He was refusing to act as a witness against himself. A right that Ernesto Miranda was not told of at his arrest. Lilburne would not incriminate himself. He was whisked away and whipped, fined, and imprisoned. Four years later, Lilburne was released when the English government declared his treatment illegal.[1]

Lilburne's famous case was one of the first cases in "due process" development. Due process means fair treatment through the judicial system that is an entitlement of every citizen. It guarantees that an individual shall be told of the charges made and that the individual shall be given the opportunity for personal defense—two things Miranda was denied. In addition, due process protection provides that action by a state must be consistent with the fundamental principles of liberty and justice. This protection against self-incrimination was a cornerstone in the *Miranda* case.

Another part of the *Miranda* case dealt with a suspect's Sixth Amendment right to have legal counsel for defense. The Fourteenth Amendment was also important to the case because it kept states from denying constitutional rights to an individual. Because of this amendment, no state can "deprive any person of life, liberty, or property, without due process of the law." This amendment was added to the Constitution in 1868, shortly after the Civil War ended in 1865. It was primarily created to uphold the national rights of former slaves in every state.

Rights Under State and Federal Laws

The Fifth Amendment privilege against self-incrimination and the Sixth Amendment right to an attorney at trial originally applied only to criminal cases in federal courts. Therefore, if a state law, such as murder or theft, had been violated, the Fifth and Sixth Amendments did not protect the accused. The *Miranda* case sought to apply these rights at a state level as well.

In considering a case about suspect rights, laws regarding both the federal (national) government and state government had to be weighed.

- **Federal Laws:** Some crimes violate federal statutes, which are laws written at the federal level, in Washington, DC, by members of Congress. Violations of these laws are prosecuted first in federal trial courts. Examples of federal statutes include laws against treason, federal income tax evasion, and kidnapping, when the victim is taken across state lines.

- **State Laws:** States have their own governments, courts, and constitutions. Some crimes violate state statutes, which are laws written at the individual state level by the members of the state legislature. Violations of these laws occur within the state and are prosecuted first in the state trial courts. Examples of state criminal statutes include laws against murder, theft, rape, and kidnapping, when the victim is not taken across state lines. This was the case for *Miranda*.

Over many decades, however, the United States Supreme Court would recognize that Fifth and Sixth Amendment rights applied at the state level. This was essential to Ernesto Miranda's case. His case concerning Fifth Amendment right would likely never have made it to the United States Supreme Court in the 1960s. His kidnap and rape charges were violations of state statutes, not federal.

An Influential Report on Police Brutality

Decades before the *Miranda* case, the United States was taking a serious look at how confessions were being obtained by law officers. In the 1930s, the way some police were extracting confessions had become a national scandal. In 1931, the National Commission on Law Observance and Enforcement, also known as the "Wickersham Commission," examined the brutality used in extracting confessions.

> Commission investigators had documented hundreds of examples of beatings, pistol whippings, strappings, lynching threats, solitary confinement in rat-infested jail cells, application of the "water cure"—holding a suspect's head under water for long periods—and protracted [very lengthy] questioning, all in an effort to elicit confessions for offenses that ranged from murder to stealing a hog.[2]

The commission's conclusion in the Wickersham Report stated, "It is not admissible to do a great right by doing a little wrong ... It is not sufficient to do justice by obtaining a proper result by irregular or improper means."[3] This report gave a whole new meaning to the phrase "The end does not justify the means." The commission recognized that a "not inconsiderable portion" of suspects who were put through such harsh treatment "are innocent."

Before the Wickersham Report, the philosophy of the United States Supreme Court centered on a "hands-off" doctrine with respect to overturning state criminal court decisions. What was the reasoning behind this doctrine? Because the states were allowed to make their own laws, they should be permitted to handle the enforcement of those laws on their own, through their state courts, without the interference of the United States Supreme Court.

After the Wickersham Report, however, the Supreme Court's philosophy began to change. Brutal cases came to the attention of the justices. No longer would it seem appropriate to step back and exercise a "hands-off" posture. The Fourteenth Amendment to the Constitution guaranteed fairness to all Americans. Supreme Court justices found that the Fourteenth Amendment due process rights were being violated; confessions were being extracted in unfair, unjust ways.

The Fourteenth Amendment, Section 1, states: "[N]or shall any State deprive any person of life, liberty, or property, without due process of law … " This amendment requires fundamental fairness, meaning that cruel or arbitrary procedures must be avoided.

Powell v. Alabama: Fair Representation

The Fourteenth Amendment has been of great importance throughout legal history in the United States. As early as 1932,

Here protestors march in defense of the "Scottsboro Boys," who were falsely accused of rape and denied their legal right to counsel.

the case of *Powell v. Alabama* came before the United States Supreme Court. In that case, often known as the "Scottsboro Nine" case, nine minority males were charged with the rape of two Caucasian girls. The accused were not told they could hire lawyers or contact their families. They had no access to a lawyer until shortly before trial, so they had little or no time to plan the defense.

In the state court, the judge appointed all the lawyers in the courtroom to represent the nine defendants. (Powell was the name of one of the defendants.) All but two attorneys withdrew from the case. And the two remaining had no opportunity to investigate on behalf of their clients. The attorneys consulted with their clients for only thirty minutes before going to trial. Eight of the defendants were convicted and sentenced to death. The jury was unable to make a decision as to the ninth defendant.

The eight defendants who were convicted appealed on the grounds that they did not get adequate legal counsel. For the first time, the United States Supreme Court overturned a state criminal court conviction due to an unfair trial. The Court used the Fourteenth Amendment as the basis for its decision. Because the poor defendants, those people unable to afford to hire an attorney for themselves, had not truly had the aid of attorneys who could help with their defense, the Court ruled that the defendants did not have due process of law. The result was that the defendants had not been granted fundamental fairness; thus, their convictions were violations of the Fourteenth Amendment.[4]

Had the Supreme Court not stepped in and ruled regarding this state court criminal trial, Ernesto Miranda's case could never have made it to the highest court in the land.

It is important to consider United States Supreme Court decisions such as *Powell v. Alabama* because each one sets a precedent. A precedent is a legal decision providing a rule of law that should be observed in future cases with the same or very similar facts. For this reason, Supreme Court decisions make a forceful impact on the future of our country.

Brown v. Mississippi: Use of Violence for a Confession

In the 1930s, the Supreme Court decided several significant cases concerning criminal justice and fair trials in addition to *Powell v. Alabama*. *Brown v. Mississippi* addressed the concern of how confessions are obtained.

On March 30, 1934 in Mississippi, a deputy sheriff discovered that a white farmer, Raymond Stewart, had been murdered in his home in Kemper County. That night, the deputy and two companions arrived at the home of Yank Ellington, a local African American man, and demanded that he come with them. They also detained two other African American men, Ed Brown and Henry Shields. The officers brought Ellington to the house of the murder victim. A mob began to shout accusations at Ellington. Ellington maintained his innocence. The mob grabbed him, dragged him to a nearby tree, and hanged him by a rope tied to a limb of the tree. Still alive, Ellington, was let down. When asked to confess, he still denied having committed the crime. The mob hanged him again from the tree limb and whipped him as he dangled in the air.

When Ellington was let down the second time, his neck was burned from the ropes that had eaten into his flesh. He continued to proclaim his innocence. The mob then tied him to a tree and whipped him. He still refused to confess. The mob finally released Ellington. In "intense pain and agony," he managed to return to his home.

Two days later, the deputy came to arrest Ellington. The two men took a long route to the police station, actually driving through another state. On the way, the deputy stopped and severely whipped Ellington, telling him that the whipping would continue until he agreed to confess. His will broken and his body in great pain, Ellington finally agreed to confess to the murder, and the deputy took him to the police station.

At the station, two other men—Brown and Shields—were accused as accomplices in the crime. They were forced to strip and were laid over chairs. Their backs were "cut to pieces with a leather strap with buckles on it," and they were threatened with more punishment until they confessed. They were tortured until every detail of their confessions matched the details "desired by the mob."[5]

In times past, confessions were routinely "beaten out of" suspects, and the right to an attorney for the accused in a criminal trial was not available in all situations. Ernesto Miranda's case occurred after decades of legal battles focusing on the rights of the accused.

When the *Brown* trial began and the defendants appeared in the courtroom, their wounds were clearly visible. And witnesses admitted having beaten the defendants. Even so, the confessions were accepted, and the defendants were sentenced to death by hanging.

The death sentence was not carried out because the Supreme Court, shocked at the methods used to obtain the confessions, reversed the convictions. Just as it had in the *Powell v. Alabama* decision, the Court based its ruling on the Fourteenth Amendment, which was quite significant in cases of this type. The Court found that confessions obtained through beatings "violated the fundamental right to a fair trial," that "the rack and torture chamber may not be substituted for the witness stand." The case determined that involuntary confession that is extracted by police violence cannot be entered as evidence. Still, the Supreme Court decision clearly stated that the self-incrimination clause of the Fifth Amendment did not apply to the states, that the decision in *Brown v. Mississippi* was based on the Fourteenth Amendment, not the Fifth Amendment.[6]

The *Brown* decision played a meaningful role in the legal history of the United States in establishing rights for the accused and how confession could be obtained. Still, in the 1930s, at the time of the *Brown* opinion, the Fifth Amendment privilege against self-incrimination and the Sixth Amendment right to an attorney had not been applied to cases in state courts.

Before the *Brown* case, the Supreme Court had generally not reviewed state cases that dealt with the admission of confessions into court. As a result, convictions at the state level generally became final. Also, before the *Brown* opinion, the courts had been much more concerned with the so-called truth of the confession than with the manner in which the confession had been obtained.

The "Voluntariness" Test

Given the atmosphere in the country and the impact of the Wickersham Report, the Supreme Court, in the *Brown* case, began to take a new look at laws governing confessions. From that time on, a new test would develop, one that Ernesto Miranda's confession would later pass in the state court.

This new test would come to be known as the "voluntariness" or "totality of the circumstances" test. In determining whether a confession had passed the test, the court would weigh the factors that determine the suspect's ability to resist police coercion. Factors such as age, intellect, education, and prior experience with the police would be weighed against physical brutality, threats, withholding of food or sleep, and long periods of questioning.

This equation would result in a decision regarding the "voluntariness" of the confession. Using the balancing test, a judge would determine whether the confession was voluntary, that is, given without coercion. If so, the confession could be heard in court and considered when determining whether the defendant was to be found guilty. If found to be involuntary, the confession could not be heard in court. It could not be used to determine whether the defendant was to be found guilty.[7]

One Supreme Court justice explained the reasoning behind the test by stating, "What would be overpowering to the weak of will ... might be utterly ineffective against an experienced criminal."[8] The justice's support for the voluntariness test was clear.

Other Supreme Court justices, such as Justice Hugo L. Black and Justice William O. Douglas, both of whom would go on to champion Ernesto Miranda's cause, found this voluntariness balancing approach totally inappropriate. They believed that a case-by-case approach was vague and unfair. The trial courts were given too much freedom in determining how to apply the test under the Fourteenth Amendment.

How could it be that two suspects who were treated exactly the same by the police during questioning could have totally opposite outcomes regarding their confessions, the justices considered. What if different state court judges weighed the factors differently?[9]

Though confession law had evolved dramatically from the days when the Supreme Court generally did not even consider state confession cases, dissatisfaction with the law remained. It is true that the *Brown* case and many cases that followed were instrumental in protecting the rights of the accused and in forming the backbone of confession law in the United States. The voluntariness test, however, failed to provide a uniform test to protect the constitutional rights of suspects accused of crimes. And still, the United States Supreme Court had yet to deal with many issues from the state level, issues such as the right to remain silent and the right of the accused to have an attorney after being taken into custody, prior to the time of the trial.

Gideon v. Wainwright: Legal Representation for the Poor

Then, in 1963, the United States Supreme Court opinion in the landmark case of *Gideon v. Wainwright* applied the Sixth Amendment, the right to counsel, to state criminal court proceedings. Before this case, not all defendants in state court trials had the right to be represented by an attorney. A state could write its own law granting the right to an attorney, but if it did not, this right generally did not exist (except in rare circumstances) because the Sixth Amendment applied only to proceedings in federal courts, not to those in state courts.

Clarence Earl Gideon's appeal to the US Supreme Court was a stepping-stone toward assuring the protection of the rights of the accused in the United States.

Thus, in a state court criminal proceeding, if the defendant wanted a lawyer but was poor and could not afford a lawyer, the judge was generally under no obligation to appoint an attorney to represent the accused.

The *Gideon* decision would change that. Clarence Earl Gideon was on trial for breaking and entering a poolroom. He asked that the judge appoint an attorney to represent him, as he was indigent. The state court judge refused to appoint a lawyer, commenting that this was not the practice in the county.

Upon appeal, the justices of the Supreme Court made it the practice and brought the United States one step closer to its opinion in the *Miranda* case. In a unanimous decision, the Court applied the Sixth Amendment, through the Fourteenth Amendment, to the states.[10] From that time forward, the law required that a lawyer be appointed to represent the poor defendant charged with a felony, an offense punishable by a year or more in prison. In 1972, the United States Supreme Court would extend the poor's right to counsel in *any* case where the defendant was sentenced to imprisonment, even if for one day.[11]

The *Gideon* opinion was a necessary stepping-stone for Ernesto Miranda's case, which dealt with the right to have an attorney during interrogation before the time of trial.

Questionable Questioning Techniques

During the 1960s, the decade of the *Gideon* decision, new and different concerns regarding confessions became evident. Even though some of the more brutal physical methods of

Here a detective questions a suspect. As you can see an interrogation could be an intense experience.

questioning had diminished somewhat, other methods became popular. These underhanded tactics revolved around clever, sometimes less obvious psychological approaches.

A former district attorney recalled a particular station house interrogation scene from the 1960s. Officers were trying to get a suspect to make a statement. The officers told the suspect to remove his clothing. The suspect bravely removed his shirt, his pants, his shoes, his socks, but not his underwear. When officers told him to remove his underwear, he refused. Rather than strip bare, the suspect asked, "What do you want to know?"[12]

Though confessions gained from this type of questioning did not involve physical brutality, they imposed another type of pressure. The suspect's constitutional rights and the protection of these rights remained complex and critical issues.

Malloy v. Hogan: Self-Incrimination on the State Level

In 1964, just after the *Gideon* decision, the Supreme Court handed down its opinion in the *Malloy v. Hogan* case, another significant break for Ernesto Miranda. In this case, William Malloy had been called upon to testify in a state hearing regarding gambling and other crimes. Malloy was on probation (subject to a period of good behavior under supervision) for a gambling offense in Connecticut. During the state hearing, he refused to answer questions regarding his earlier arrest and conviction, asserting his Fifth Amendment privilege against self-incrimination. Malloy was held in contempt of court, ordered to prison, and told he would remain there until he agreed to answer.

The Supreme Court ruled that Malloy's constitutional rights had been violated. The justices utilized the Fourteenth Amendment to apply the Fifth Amendment privilege against self-incrimination to state court proceedings. No longer would the Fifth Amendment privilege against self-incrimination be denied to defendants in state courts.[13]

The *Malloy* case would be a huge piece of the foundation for Ernesto Miranda's argument. Still, all the necessary Supreme Court decisions were not yet in place to lead to the future reversal of Miranda's state court conviction. Important issues, such as the right to an attorney during interrogation and the right to remain silent after arrest, had yet to be ruled upon in a light favorable to Miranda.

Escobedo v. Illinois: **Right to an Attorney**

Shortly after the *Gideon* and *Malloy* decisions, Danny Escobedo's landmark case would truly pave the way for Ernesto Miranda.

In 1960, twenty-two-year-old Danny Escobedo was living in Chicago. In the early hours of a cold winter morning, he was picked up by police officers and taken in for questioning. Escobedo's brother-in-law had been murdered several hours earlier. Escobedo made no statement and, through his attorney's efforts, was released.

Ten days later, Escobedo was again arrested, this time with his sister-in-law, the victim's widow. In the car, on the way to the police station, officers gave Escobedo a piece of startling news. Escobedo should confess, they advised, because his good friend, Benedict DiGerlando, had already told them the "truth," that Escobedo had fired the fatal shots.

Keeping his wits, Escobedo did not offer a statement, but asked for his lawyer. Escobedo's lawyer arrived at the police station. The lawyer saw his client through the occasionally opened door of the interrogation room, but the police refused to let Escobedo's

---

Danny Escobedo had served four and a half years of his sentence when he was freed after the Supreme Court's decision on his case.

lawyer in the room with him. They hoped to get a confession and thought the lawyer would interfere. At one point, the two even waved to each other.

Still, repeated requests by Escobedo and his attorney to confer were denied. Finally, the lawyer left to file a complaint with the Chicago police commissioner.

A short time later, DiGerlando was brought into the interrogation room by police. Escobedo shouted, "I didn't shoot Manuel. You did it!"

The police finally obtained a signed confession from Escobedo. He admitted having paid DiGerlando $500 to commit the murder.

At the trial in state court, Escobedo denied his confession. He said that he had been tricked into making it, and that the police had promised he would be released and would not be prosecuted if he would just sign the confession form.

The confession was not thrown out. Escobedo was sentenced to life in prison. He appealed his conviction. When his appeal reached the United States Supreme Court, his conviction was reversed. The Court's opinion stated that Escobedo should have been granted the right to speak to his attorney upon request, that he had been denied his constitutional rights under the Sixth and Fourteenth Amendments.[14]

In ruling on Escobedo's appeal, the Supreme Court utilized the Fourteenth Amendment to apply the Sixth Amendment right to counsel, just as the Court had done in the *Gideon* case. In the *Escobedo* decision, however, the Supreme Court went one step further than it had in the *Gideon* opinion. With *Gideon*, the Court decided that the accused has the right to a lawyer at his or her trial. With *Escobedo*, the Court ruled that the suspect had the right to have a requested attorney present prior to the time of trial, during questioning. Miranda's case would take this idea a step farther: The accused had to be notified that he or she had a right to an attorney, and if the accused could not afford one, the court would appoint one for the accused.

A Country Divided

In the 1960s, at the time of the *Gideon* and *Escobedo* decisions, the Supreme Court was often referred to as the "Warren Court," since its chief justice then was Earl Warren. So-called "liberals," who strongly supported the civil rights of the individual, supported the Supreme Court with equal force.

A division had been forming in the country, however. Some Americans felt that the Supreme Court was falling off of its tightrope in the balancing act of protecting individual rights versus protecting society's or victims' rights.

The Court had upheld civil rights by declaring segregation in schools unconstitutional. Further, the Court had disturbed local political practices by ordering changes regarding voting districts. Ever since a series of landmark rulings in the 1960s, districts have been drawn "as nearly of equal population as is practicable." These decisions angered some Americans.[15]

And many Americans were furious with the decisions of the Court regarding the rights of the accused. Decisions such as *Powell*, *Brown*, *Gideon*, and *Malloy* were particular sore spots for these critics. And they became even more distressed when the *Escobedo* decision was handed down.

The *Escobedo* decision set off waves of anger and fear through various segments of the American public. Some Americans believed the Supreme Court had bent over backward to protect the rights of the criminal but had forgotten the rights of the victim, and of society at large. Other Americans cheered the way the Supreme Court had defended the rights of the accused. If the *Escobedo* decision deepened a division already created by earlier Supreme Court decisions, then the *Miranda* ruling would surely rip the country apart and create a valley between opponents in this constitutional clash.

Though the country was sharply divided, there could be no doubt that the *Powell, Brown, Gideon, Malloy,* and *Escobedo* decisions were all moving the needle in favor of Ernesto Miranda. Each set a new precedent and shed new light on the interpretation of constitutional rights for the accused in a criminal case.

CHAPTER 3
Making a Case for Miranda

Defending Ernesto Miranda and appealing his case to the Supreme Court would not be easy. The eighth-grade dropout was a known criminal. He had been in trouble with the law since age fourteen. When he allegedly raped Rebecca Ann Johnson at age twenty-three, he already had a prior arrest record for armed robbery, attempted rape, burglary, and assault.[1]

Even as a child, Miranda led a troubled life. When he was six years old, his mother died. His father, a house painter, remarried the following year, and Miranda battled often with his stepmother. He soon lost close contact with his brothers, and with his father, whom he said had beaten him.

As a student at Queen of Peace Catholic School in Mesa, Arizona, Miranda was a nightmare for the nuns and priests. He was absent more than he was present, and he created more than his share of disciplinary problems.

In 1954, Miranda finished the eighth grade. That same year, he was arrested for his first felony, auto theft, for which he was put on probation. He returned to school the following year, but dropped out.

In 1955, he was arrested for burglary and sentenced to serve time in the Arizona State Industrial School for Boys. The strict disciplinary measures at the State Boys' School did not stop Miranda from breaking laws, either. He returned home in December of 1955, and one month later, he was arrested for rape and assault. He was sent back to the State Boys' School for one year.

Again, this time in jail did little, if anything, to stop Miranda from pursuing illegal activities. Between 1956 and 1961, he was convicted and imprisoned in Arizona, California, Texas, Tennessee, and Ohio for a variety of crimes. During that time, he served in the United States Army, where he went AWOL (absent without official leave, or permission), much in line with his behavior in grammar school years before. His future brushes with the law would include a number of arrests for transporting cars across state lines. He would later say that he stole cars because he was "too lazy to work."

In 1962, Miranda was between jail sentences and settled in the Phoenix, Arizona, area with Twila Hoffman. She would later prove to be his downfall in the second Rebecca Ann Johnson kidnap-rape trial.

Hoffman went to work in a nursery school while Miranda wove his way in and out of employment. He rarely held a job for more than two weeks. Finally, in August of 1962, Miranda got a job as a truck driver for a produce company. He was well regarded by his employer. Miranda and Hoffman had a baby girl, and it looked as though Miranda might "finally settle down into a normal, respectable life."

This fleeting stability, however, would be shattered when Miranda began cruising the Phoenix area, and committing a number of crimes against women. These included kidnap, rape, and robbery. The exact number of victims will never be known. Rebecca Ann Johnson was among them.[2]

Miranda's Arrest

On March 13, 1963, Miranda had worked all night long. One hour after he had arrived home and gone to sleep, Phoenix police officers Cooley and Young appeared at his door.

They asked Miranda to accompany them to the police station to answer some questions about a case they were investigating. Miranda later explained, "I didn't know whether I had a choice. I got in the car and asked them what it was about. They said they couldn't tell me anything."[3]

At the police station, officers put Miranda in a lineup with three other men. Rebecca Ann was not able to identify any of them as her attacker, but she believed Miranda's build and features were similar to those of the man who had kidnapped and raped her. She asked if she could hear Miranda speak, believing that she could identify his voice.[4]

From the lineup, Miranda was taken to an interrogation room, where he asked the officers, "How did I do?"

"You flunked," they answered.[5]

When the interrogation began, no attorney was present to protect Miranda's constitutional rights. Before the

This photograph of arresting officer Carroll F. Cooley is on display at the Phoenix Police Museum.

questioning began, Miranda was not told that he had the right to an attorney, and a dispute existed as to whether he had been told he had the right to remain silent.

Rebecca Ann Johnson was brought to the interrogation room, and officers asked Miranda to state his name and address so that Rebecca Ann could hear his voice. Officers then pointed to Rebecca Ann Johnson and asked Miranda, "Is that the girl?"

Believing that he had already been identified by the victim in the lineup, Miranda replied, "That's the girl."

As soon as Rebecca Ann heard Miranda's voice, she was certain that he was the man who had kidnapped and raped her.

Confessing to the Crime

During a relatively short interrogation period, Miranda not only confessed to the crime against Rebecca Ann Johnson, but admitted a robbery as well.

Officers were ready to get Miranda's statement in writing. They gave him a typed confession form. Near the top of the page appeared the statement:

I,_____, do hereby swear that I make this statement voluntarily and of my own free will, with no threats, coercion, or promises of immunity, and with full knowledge of my legal rights, understanding any statement I make may be used against me.

Miranda signed his name in the blank, wrote his confession, and signed at the bottom. Although the form stated that Miranda's confession was made with full knowledge of his rights, records reflect that officers did not explain exactly what those rights were.[6]

Miranda's State Trial

In June 1963, the trial in the case of *The State of Arizona v. Ernesto Miranda* got under way in an Arizona state court.

Miranda's lawyer, seventy-three-year-old Alvin Moore, had been appointed by the court. He was paid $100 to defend Miranda in this case.[7]

Because Miranda had signed a confession, Moore did not see much hope for his case. He decided that the best approach would be to argue that Miranda was insane at the time of the rape. In an attempt to prove this, Moore asked the court to appoint two psychiatrists to examine his client. Neither found Miranda insane, but they did find that Miranda was immature and emotionally ill. Still, both doctors believed that he knew the difference between right and wrong. Their written opinions stated that Miranda knew the nature and consequences of his acts and that he was able to understand the proceedings against him and to assist in his own defense.[8]

Miranda's attorney did not really like his client, but he did believe he had certain legal rights that had to be upheld. He told the jury, "You know, perhaps a doctor doesn't enjoy operating for locked bowels, but he has to."[9]

So, to provide proper legal representation for his client, Moore objected to Miranda's confession. He tried to keep Miranda's confession from being admitted as evidence, so that the jury could neither hear nor see it.

To make a legal objection, Moore has to state the grounds, or legal basis, for his motion. Moore based his objection on the Sixth Amendment's right to counsel. "We object because the Supreme Court of the United States says a man is entitled to an attorney at the time of his arrest," Moore stated.[10] Moore used this reasoning to uphold Miranda's right to have a lawyer present during the interrogation, before the trial. In reality, the Supreme Court had not yet made this ruling at the time of Miranda's trial. The *Escobedo* decision, which would state that the accused had a right to an attorney before the trial, would not be established until about a year after the *Miranda* trial in June of 1964.

How Miranda's Confession Was Given

When Officers Cooley and Young testified at Miranda's trial regarding the confession, they admitted that no explanation of rights had been given. Because they were aware that Miranda was an ex-convict, they believed that he knew his rights. Miranda had been through the "routine" before, lawyers would later argue, so there was no need to explain his rights in detail.

Further, Cooley and Young testified that neither threats nor promises had been made in exchange for Miranda's confession to the crime of rape. It was given without coercion when they had questioned him. [11]

Miranda's account of his interrogation, though not stated at the trial, was quite different.

Once they get you in a little room and they start badgering you one way or the other, "You better tell us … or we're going to throw the book at you," … that is what was told to me. They would throw the book at me. They would try to give me all the time [in prison] they could. They thought there was even the possibility that there was something wrong with me.

They would try to help me, get me medical care if I needed it …
And I haven't had any sleep since the day before. I'm tired. I just
got off work, and they have me and they are interrogating me.
They mention first one crime, then another one, (sic) they are
certain I am the person … knowing what a penitentiary is like,
a person has to be frightened, scared. And not knowing if he'll
be able to get back up and go home.[12]

When it was time for the judge in Miranda's trial to rule on
the admissibility (whether evidence will be heard or excluded)
of the confession, he allowed the confession into evidence.[13] This
ruling meant that Moore's objection was overruled, and the jury
was allowed to consider Miranda's confession when deciding
whether to find him guilty or not guilty.

The Road to the Supreme Court

Miranda was convicted and sentenced to twenty to thirty years in
prison. He was shipped off to the Arizona State prison farm. There
he became best known as a barber, not as the celebrated "right-to-
remain-silent man" he would become after his case had traveled to
the highest court in the land.[14]

After this Arizona State trial, Miranda's case was appealed to
the Arizona Supreme Court. Miranda awaited the state supreme
court's ruling from his prison cell. After almost a year and a half,
the conviction was upheld, or left in place. The Arizona State
Supreme Court stated that Miranda already knew his rights, since
he was an ex-convict.[15]

Following the Arizona Supreme Court's decision in Miranda's case, the American Civil Liberties Union (ACLU) became interested in his rights and the legal complexities of the case.

Robert Corcoran, the ACLU lawyer, was very concerned about Miranda's constitutional rights. According to Corcoran, an appeal to the United States Supreme Court was warranted. The *Escobedo* case, which stated that the suspect had the right to a requested attorney during questioning, would be an important aspect of the appeal.

After the *Escobedo* ruling, many unsuccessful attempts had been made to expand the constitutional rights of the accused. Attorney Corcoran, who would later become an Arizona Supreme Court justice, believed that Ernesto Miranda's case might just be the appeal that could succeed.[16]

Corcoran's frustration regarding the United States Supreme Court's failure to expand the rights of the accused mirrored the dissatisfaction of many Americans who wanted to see an expansion of the constitutional rights of the criminal suspect. The *Escobedo* decision had provided new rights for the accused, rights that had not existed before. Prior to *Escobedo*, the accused in a state court proceeding was entitled to an attorney at the time of trial—not before. In the *Escobedo* decision, the United States Supreme Court expanded the right to an attorney. This right became available at the time of interrogation, before the trial.

Even though, in the minds of those who supported expansion of the rights of the accused, the *Escobedo* case had made a giant step forward in constitutional law, further steps had met a brick wall.

Lawyers Take the Case

Miranda's attorney, Moore, was not in a position to handle his client's appeal to the United States Supreme Court, so Corcoran approached the law firm of Lewis, Roca, Scoville, Beauchamps & Linton. Two lawyers there, John Flynn and John Frank, volunteered to take the case pro bono, or free of charge. Frank was a graduate of the University of Wisconsin and Yale Law School. He had served as a law clerk to United States Supreme Court Justice Hugo Black, and had taught law at Yale. Flynn, a former World War II combat marine with a law degree from the University of Arizona was "acknowledged as one of the most astute criminal lawyers in the state [Arizona]."[17] In July of 1965, they petitioned the Supreme Court to hear the case. The Court usually hears cases that could have national significance. In November of that year, the Court agreed to hear the case along with three other cases involving confessions made during police interrogations.

At first, Flynn and Frank disagreed about the major legal point for the appeal. Flynn wanted to base the appeal on the Fifth Amendment privilege against self-incrimination. According to him, the circumstances surrounding Miranda's interrogation made the confession invalid. Upon appeal, he would put forth the position that Miranda was entitled to be made aware of his rights. Flynn asserted that at the time of questioning during

Ernesto Miranda is shown talking to John Flynn here.

the investigation, Miranda should have had the opportunity to assert his Fifth Amendment privilege against self-incrimination.

Miranda's other lawyer, Frank, wanted to base the appeal on the Sixth Amendment right to counsel. His argument centered on the fact that, regardless of whether or not Miranda asked for an attorney, he had the right to representation at the time of questioning.

Ultimately, the Sixth Amendment position won out. The Sixth Amendment would be the basis for Ernesto Miranda's appeal to the Supreme Court of the United States.

Gideon and *Escobedo* Paved the Way

It was true that the *Gideon* and *Escobedo* cases, which had been decided in time to be of benefit in Miranda's appeal, had not spelled out specifically that an accused must be advised of the right to an attorney before questioning. Still, Miranda's lawyers would make a strong appeal that the Sixth Amendment did provide that right and that the *Gideon* and *Escobedo* decisions had led the Court in this direction.[18]

Constitutional law is quite complex. Although the choice between Fifth Amendment and Sixth Amendment arguments might not always seem clear-cut, it is important for lawyers to choose a position upon which to base an appeal. Once the position has been chosen, attorneys can research the law as it relates to the specific points of the appeal. Only then can the lawyers discuss precedent to support their positions.

Writing the Brief

The brief, or written legal argument, for *Miranda* was clear and to the point. Miranda's lawyers framed their arguments in persuasive, simple, direct terms. The brief detailed Miranda's lineup and identification, his interrogation, and his confession. Lawyers discussed their opinions of the *Escobedo* decision as it applied to Miranda's case. They stated that the Arizona Supreme Court had given the *Escobedo* case "such a narrow construction that, for all practical purposes, the protections of the Sixth Amendment are not available to those persons so unaware of their rights or so intimidated that they do not request 'the guiding hand of counsel' at this crucial stage."

In addition, the lawyers stated their concern over giving "the knowledgeable suspect … a constitutional preference over those members of society most in need of assistance." The lawyers were concerned that certain members of society who are wealthy or well-educated might have an "edge" over those who are poor and illiterate. The wealthy and well-educated would likely know that they should request an attorney. The poor and illiterate, who truly need the protection of the Constitution, might not be aware of their rights.

Frank and Flynn asked, in their brief, whether "the confession of a poorly educated, mentally abnormal, indigent defendant, not told of his right to counsel, taken while he is in police custody and without the assistance of counsel, which was never requested, can be admitted into evidence over specific objection based on the absence of counsel?"

The lawyers went on to discuss past cases that had dealt with issues such as the coerced confession and the right to counsel. They brought up cases such as *Powell v. Alabama, Brown v. Mississippi,* and *Gideon v. Wainwright.* Particularly, the lawyers quoted from the *Powell v. Alabama* decision, stating that, under the due process clause of the Fourteenth Amendment, the criminal defendant was entitled to the "guiding hand of counsel in every step of the proceedings against him."

The lawyers argued whether the Sixth Amendment right to counsel, as applied to the states through the Fourteenth Amendment, gave the same right to have counsel at interrogation as at the time of trial. In answering this question, Flynn and Frank stated that this right did exist, not as the result of the

Escobedo ruling, or of any other single case, but rather because "there is a tide in the affairs of men, and it is this engulfing tide which is washing away the secret interrogation of the unprotected accused."

The *Escobedo* opinion, Miranda's lawyers argued, had already recognized the interrogation as a proceeding covered by the Sixth Amendment. Thus, the poor suspect did have the right to counsel during interrogation, whether counsel had been requested or not.

Flynn and Frank closed their brief with a powerful point: "We invoke the basic principles of *Powell v. Alabama*: 'He requires the guiding hand of counsel at every step in the proceeding against him.' When Miranda stepped into Interrogation Room 2, he had only the guiding hand of Officers Cooley and Young."[19]

Miranda's attorneys had made their arguments. The lawyer for the state of Arizona had a few of his own.

CHAPTER 4

Arizona's Argument Against Miranda

While Miranda's lawyers built a case to defend the suspect's rights, the state of Arizona had to build a case that their methods were in the best interest of bringing justice for the victim and fairly bringing a suspect to trial. Many organizations thought the *Miranda* case would favor the alleged criminal too much, and they submitted *amicus curiae* ("friend of the court") briefs warning the Supreme Court that the *Miranda* ruling could interfere with police interrogations. Arizona would be arguing that although they did not tell Miranda about his right to a lawyer, they never denied a request for one and they never threatened him or physically assaulted him to get a confession. A look back months before Ernesto Miranda's trial helps us to understand how Arizona developed its side of the case.

At this time, prosecutors in the Maricopa County Attorney's Office in Phoenix, Arizona, received police reports regarding the kidnap-rape of Rebecca Ann Johnson.[1] Reports were sent to his office because a criminal case is generally prosecuted in the county where the crime occurred, and in this case the incident happened in Maricopa County.

Lawyers working in the county attorney's office represent the people of the state of Arizona. The victims in their criminal cases are referred to as "complaining witnesses" and do not have to pay a fee for representation. This money is generally paid through tax dollars. Rebecca Ann Johnson was the complaining witness in the *Miranda* case.

Before the trial, prosecutors had at their disposal over twenty pages of police reports, not to mention many other records in the case.[2] Miranda had been convicted of robbery the day before his trial in the Rebecca Ann Johnson kidnap-rape case. He had confessed to that robbery at the same time he confessed to the kidnap-rape.[3]

On June 20, 1963, Ernesto Miranda's trial for the kidnap-rape of Rebecca Ann Johnson began. Attorneys chose the jury members and began presenting testimony, questioning witnesses.

Prosecutors questioned a total of four witnesses: complaining witness Rebecca Ann Johnson, Rebecca Ann's sister, and Officers Cooley and Young.[4]

Rebecca Ann Johnson was the first witness called to the stand. She sometimes had to stop speaking and take a break since her voice was trembling.[5] She did, however, identify Ernesto Miranda from the witness stand, as the man who had kidnapped and raped her.

After Rebecca Ann stepped down from the stand, her sister testified. Her sister's testimony centered on Rebecca Ann's condition at the time she had arrived home. "She came home, pounded on the door, her hair was all over like she had been in a fight, and her dress was brand new, a new suit, and it was a mess, and she was crying and carrying on, and I asked her what was the matter ... " Rebecca Ann's sister was questioned only briefly by the prosecutor. Miranda's lawyer asked her no questions.

The prosecutor next called Officer Cooley, and then Officer Young to the stand. They testified for quite some time, detailing the crime as it had been described to them. They also testified as to the lineup and Miranda's confession.

On cross-examination, Miranda's lawyer asked about how the confession had been obtained:

Question: Did you warn him of his rights?

Answer: Yes, Sir.

Question: But did you ever, before or during your conversation or before taking this statement, did you ever advise the defendant he was entitled to the services of an attorney?

Answer: When I read—

Question: Before he made any statement?

Answer: When I read the statement right there.

Question: I don't see in the statement that it says where he is entitled to the services of an attorney before he made it.

Answer: No, sir.

Question: Is it not in that statement?

Answer: It doesn't say anything about an attorney ...

Question: … It is not your practice to advise people you arrest that they are entitled to the services of an attorney before they make a statement?

Answer: No, sir.

Moore, Miranda's court-appointed lawyer, tried to keep the jury from hearing the confession, objecting on the grounds that his client's rights had been violated because Miranda had not had an attorney present at the time the confession was made. The objection was overruled, and the jury was allowed to consider the confession.

Miranda's lawyer presented no defense witnesses; Miranda did not take the stand. The prosecutor and the defense attorney made their final arguments to the jury.

All in all, the trial had been quite short, and the legal arguments had been confined to a minimum amount of time.

Establishing a Reasonable Doubt

After the final arguments, the judge instructed the jury about the law. He told the jurors that in order to convict Miranda, they would have to find that the state had proven its case beyond a reasonable doubt.[6]

"Beyond a reasonable doubt" is the burden of proof required of the prosecution in a criminal case. This means that jurors or judge believe that the evidence shows with certainty that no alternative is possible. Many people believe that a criminal case must be proven "beyond a shadow of a doubt" rather than a reasonable doubt.

This idea has been promoted by television shows and movies, but it is not the standard used by the courts. In order to believe a case beyond a shadow of a doubt, a jury would, at the very least, need to view a videotape of a crime. Except in the rarest or most bizarre of circumstances, this simply does not happen. And the prosecutor cannot physically return the jurors to the crime scene on the date at the time the offense occurred.

This is the highest standard that must be met in any trial. This standard of proof is higher than in a civil case. A civil case is typically a dispute between individuals or entities such as a corporation or the government. The argument is usually about a responsibility one party owes the other. The primary purpose of civil law is to provide compensation (usually money) for someone or an entity wronged by the acts or behaviors of another. Criminal laws, on the other hand, punish those who commit acts that deemed undesirable by society—such as murder, robbery, and rape. The standard of proof in a civil case is to present a "preponderance of evidence." This means that the evidence presented convinces the court that it's more likely than not that the plaintiff's accusation is true. (A plaintiff is a person who brings a case against another in a court of law.)

In a criminal case, a person can be deprived of liberty and can be left with a criminal record. So the outcomes of a criminal case are vastly different from a civil case.

In the *Miranda* trial, the judge instructed the jury regarding reasonable doubt in this way:

A reasonable doubt is not a mere whim or guess or imaginary doubt, nor is it a mere subterfuge [trick] to which resort may be held in order to avoid doing a disagreeable thing. It is such a doubt as reasonable men may entertain after a careful and honest review and consideration of all the evidence in the case. It must be founded in reason and common sense.

Regarding Miranda's failure to testify in the trial, the judge instructed the jury:

It is a constitutional right of a defendant in a criminal trial that he may not be compelled to testify. Thus whether or not he does testify rests entirely in his own decision. The failure of a defendant to deny or explain evidence against him does not create a presumption of guilt, nor does it relieve the prosecution of its burden of proving every essential element of the crime and the guilt of the defendant beyond a reasonable doubt.

The judge went on to instruct the jurors regarding the law as it relates to confessions. The jurors were told that it was their job to determine whether Ernesto Miranda's confession had been made voluntarily. If so, the confession could be considered.

If, however, the jurors found the confession to have been made *involuntarily,* they were told that they must entirely *disregard* it and not consider it for any purpose. The judge went on to state:

A confession is involuntary when it is obtained by any sort of violence or threats, or by any direct or implied promises of immunity [protection] or benefit, or by any improper influence which might induce in the mind of the defendant the belief or hope that he would gain or benefit or be better off by making a statement, and where the defendant makes such confession as a result of any such inducement originating with a law enforcement officer. But the fact that a defendant was under arrest at the time he made a confession or that he was not at the time represented by Counsel or that he was not told that any statement that he might make could or would be used against him, in and of themselves, will not render such confession involuntary.[7]

After deliberating, or discussing the case in the jury room, for five hours, the nine-man, three-woman jury returned to the courtroom with a verdict. Ernesto Miranda was pronounced guilty of kidnap and rape.

Sentencing and Appeals

Miranda was sent to the county jail to await his sentencing. The following week, on June 27, 1963, Ernesto Miranda was summoned from jail to the courtroom. The judge sentenced him to not less than twenty years, nor more than thirty years on the kidnap conviction. He was sentenced to the same punishment, twenty to thirty years, on the rape conviction. The two sentences would, however, run concurrently (at the same time) so Miranda would be serving time in prison for both offenses at once. His total sentence in the Rebecca Ann Johnson crime would be twenty to thirty years.

Ernesto Miranda's sentence, however, would grow longer once he was sentenced for robbery as well. On June 27, 1963, he received a sentence of twenty to twenty-five years. The judge pronounced that this sentence would run consecutively (immediately following) with the kidnap-rape sentence. Thus, Miranda would be sentenced to a total of not less than forty nor more than fifty-five years in prison for the crimes against the robbery victim and Rebecca Ann Johnson.

Miranda's lawyer filed notice of intention to appeal both the robbery and the kidnap-rape convictions to the Arizona Supreme Court.[8] Appeal means to apply to a higher court for a reversal of the decision of a lower court. While Miranda's lawyer argued to the state supreme court that his client's convictions should be reversed, the lawyers for the state of Arizona strongly urged the convictions be affirmed.

The state's position was that Ernesto Miranda's confession had been voluntary and that no law existed which required that officers offer an attorney to a suspect prior to questioning. The Arizona Supreme Court agreed with the state's attorney, and on April 22, 1965, Miranda's conviction was upheld.

In examining the Sixth and Fourteenth Amendments and their guarantees, the Arizona Supreme Court spoke of the balance necessary:

[B]etween the competing interests of society and the rights of the individual ... Society has the right of protection against those who roam the streets for the purpose of violating the law, but that protection must not be at the expense of the rights of the individual guaranteed under the Sixth and Fourteenth Amendments to our Constitution.

The court emphasized, however, that Miranda had not been deprived of his constitutional rights. He had not asked for an attorney. This point was a critical one in the comparison between the United States Supreme Court's *Escobedo* decision and the facts in Ernesto Miranda's case. The Arizona Supreme Court went on to state that Miranda had "a record which indicated that he was not without courtroom experience" and that "he was certainly not unfamiliar with legal procedure and his rights in court."[9]

Arizona's Response to the Appeal

After the Arizona Supreme Court upheld Miranda's convictions, John Flynn and John Frank appealed the kidnap-rape case to the highest authority—the United States Supreme Court. When Miranda's lawyers took his kidnap-rape case to the United States Supreme Court, they decided it was not necessary to take the same steps in the robbery case. They did not appeal that case. Their reasoning was well-founded. If the justices reversed the conviction in the kidnap-rape, surely the conviction in the robbery case would not stand, as Miranda had confessed to both cases at the same time, under the same circumstances.[10]

After Miranda's appeal to the United States Supreme Court in the kidnap-rape case was filed, notice was sent to the Arizona Attorney General's Office, the office that handled appeals for the people of the state of Arizona. In the Criminal Appeals Division of the Arizona Attorney General's Office, only one assistant attorney general and a couple of law clerks handled the appeals for the state. The assistant attorney general who handled the case of *Miranda v. Arizona* was Gary Nelson.

Nelson had earned a law degree from the University of Arizona only three years before. Still, he was highly regarded, having received many honors for speaking and academic skills.[11]

It was Nelson's responsibility to handle the response of the state of Arizona to Ernesto Miranda's appeal to the Supreme Court of the United States. Nelson had no objection to the United States Supreme Court hearing the *Miranda* case. He agreed with Flynn and Frank that the legal issues presented in Miranda's case had been a source of confusion. He further stated, however, that the rights granted to the accused in the *Escobedo* case should not be expanded. Nelson was quick to point out that, in the *Escobedo* case, the defendant had asked for an attorney. Miranda had made no such request, and as a result, the Phoenix police had not made a legal error by failing to provide an attorney. In addition, Nelson stated that Escobedo had not had experience with the police, whereas Miranda had an extensive criminal record.

Nelson added that Ernesto Miranda had been questioned only by police officers in a "routine investigation." Escobedo's interrogation had been carried out by police officers and a bright state's attorney.

Nelson went on to note that Escobedo had been "tricked" into confessing when told that another person had identified

---

Gary Nelson was Arizona's assistant attorney general from 1964 to 1968 and then served as attorney general from 1968 to 1974.

him as being the man who had pulled the trigger. He pointed out that in Miranda's case, on the other hand, police officers had not used tricks.[12]

Whether or not the police officers had used tricks with Miranda was, of course, debatable. After the lineup, officers told Miranda that he had "flunked," when, in fact, he hadn't. Further, officers asked Miranda, "Is that the girl?" These tactics could be viewed as tricks.

Assistant Attorney General Nelson addressed the issue of advice given to suspects regarding constitutional rights. Escobedo had been given none. Miranda, however, had agreed in his statement that he understood his rights and waived them.

Certainly, the United States Supreme Court would consider the fact that, although Miranda signed a statement advising he was aware of his rights, these rights were never specified. He was not told that he had the right to have an attorney present. Records reflected that he was not told that he had a right to remain silent, though this matter was later disputed. It was the position of the state of Arizona, however, that these warnings simply were not necessary.

It was further the position of the state of Arizona that constitutional protections did not exist for the purpose of giving the guilty special chances for acquittal, or being found "not guilty." Furthermore, Nelson was particularly provoked by a specific comment Miranda's lawyers had made in their brief: "[Miranda] states his life, for all practical purposes, was over when he walked out of Interrogation Room #2 on March 13, 1963."

In the state's brief, Nelson replied, "The real fact is that Miranda's life was unalterably destined ten days earlier during the late evening hours of March 2 and the early morning hours of March 3, when he kidnapped and raped his victim ... "[13] Nelson's reply illustrated his irritation with blaming police officers for Ernesto Miranda's fate, and his belief that Miranda had determined his own destiny by committing the crimes against Rebecca Ann Johnson.

Miranda's lawyers, John Flynn and John Frank, had dynamically presented the appeal on behalf of their client, Ernesto Miranda. Assistant Attorney General Gary Nelson had supported his position on behalf of the people of the state of Arizona.

Now the case of *Miranda v. Arizona* was in the hands of the nine justices of the Supreme Court of the United States.

CHAPTER 5

The Supreme Court Rules

Over the course of three days from February 28 to March 2, 1966, lawyers argued their positions on *Miranda*. The justices, however, would take three months to debate the issues and finally decide if Miranda had been given fair due process of the law. The Court decision would have a major impact on how law enforcers did their job and how the accused would be treated. Many waited anxiously, and some feared that it would make police work more difficult and let many guilty parties go free. In the 1960s, crime was on the rise in America, so this was a hot button topic.

On June 13, 1966, the Supreme Court handed down its decision in the *Miranda* case to a packed courtroom. This ruling fed the fires of controversy blazing around the rights of the accused versus the rights of the victim and society. Indeed,

---

The chief justice of the Supreme Court during the *Miranda* hearing was Earl Warren. Warren was known for his liberal opinions.

the Supreme Court decision was made by the smallest possible margin, 5 to 4.

Ernesto Miranda's name became entwined with legal history almost as the luck of the draw. His case was actually ruled upon along with three others, due to the fact that all four cases involved essentially the same legal issues. Of these four cases, Miranda's was listed first because he was the first to formally request that the United States Supreme Court hear his case.[1] So, the Supreme Court decision in regard to Ernesto Miranda, Michael Vignera, Carl Calvin Westover, and Roy Allen Stewart came to be known in the history books, in the police departments, in the courtrooms, and on the streets across the country as the *Miranda* decision.

In 1966, the time was ripe for a ruling on legal issues like those presented in Miranda's case. Why then, did the Supreme Court justices have to wait for Miranda's appeal to come to them? Why could the justices not set down the law as they believed it should be?

It is true that the Supreme Court does make law when it hands down decisions. Supreme Court justices cannot, however, simply decide to make rules of law. Rather, a "case or controversy" must exist. This means that the justices must wait for an appropriate case to come to them in order to be able to rule on a particular area of the law.

Three Other Cases about Confessions

The Supreme Court heard the *Miranda* case along with three other cases related to confessions obtained during police questioning.

- **_Vignera v. New York_:** Michael Vignera was picked up in New York in connection to a robbery of a dress shop. He was questioned for eight hours, but never told he had the right to remain silent. Questioning continued after he signed a confession. Vignera, however, lost his appeal and his conviction was affirmed.

- **_Stewart v. California_:** Police in Los Angeles arrested Roy Stewart for robbery and murder. After questioning nine times over five days, he was convicted. The Supreme Court overturned his conviction, saying the interrogation method was not just.

- **_Westover v. United States_:** Law enforcers arrested Carl Westover for robbery. After two and a half hours of interrogation by the FBI, Westover signed confessions. The confession included a printed paragraph stating that he understood his rights. His conviction was upheld.[2]

Tracing the Course of the _Miranda_ Case

Initially, Ernesto Miranda's case was decided at the state court level, where he was convicted. He appealed to the Arizona Supreme Court, where his conviction was upheld. Then Miranda personally made a request from his prison cell that the United States Supreme Court hear his case. Such a request is called a petition for "writ of certiorari."

When Miranda sent his petition, he filed a pauper's form, which stated that he had little or no money and could not pay the $100 filing fee. Filing a pauper's form also meant that Miranda would be required to furnish only one petition to the United States Supreme Court, rather than the usually required forty copies.

Unfortunately, Miranda forgot to attach a statement of his inability to pay. He also forgot to attach another important document—the final judgment of the Arizona Supreme Court. As both documents were required by law, Miranda's petition was dismissed.[3]

A short time later, Arizona attorneys John Flynn and John Frank agreed to represent Miranda. Working on a pro bono basis, the lawyers contributed over $50,000 in office time alone, not including printing costs, travel time, and additional expenses.

When Flynn and Frank agreed to represent Miranda, he sent them a letter of thanks.[4] Little did Ernesto Miranda know that when he wrote that letter these two lawyers would take his case to the highest court and make it part of legal history.

Accused Rights v. Victim Rights

After Miranda's lawyers and lawyers in many other cases had submitted petitions for writ of certiorari, the Supreme Court justices began the process of deciding which cases they would hear. These were the cases in which they would grant certiorari, or a request from the Supreme Court to a lower court to send up the record of the case for review. At the time the petition in the *Miranda* case was submitted, the justices had asked their clerks to seek out *Escobedo* type cases, cases that dealt with the right to an attorney. The justices were concerned with the confusion in the country following the *Escobedo* decision.

Were the criminal suspect's constitutional rights to be expanded? After the *Escobedo* ruling, law enforcement officers knew they must provide an attorney if one was requested. But what if one had not been requested? When exactly did the right to an attorney arise? These and many other questions were being asked by people throughout the nation.[5]

Up until the *Miranda* ruling, the Supreme Court had narrowly interpreted the *Escobedo* decision. So many who thought they might have case similar to *Escobedo* were appealing but not getting reversals of their convictions. In many instances, the decisions of the state courts were allowed to stand. Those Americans on the "law and order" side of the controversy expressed approval, while those Americans on the "suspect's rights" side anxiously awaited the day when criminal suspects' constitutional rights would be made broader.

On November 22, 1965, the Supreme Court of the United States granted certiorari in Miranda's case. Shortly thereafter, the Court also agreed to hear the cases of Michael Vignera, Carl Calvin Westover, and Roy Allen Stewart—the three men whose cases were similar to Miranda's. The Court then requested briefs from the lawyers in those cases. Briefs are written legal arguments stating the reasons for the suit based on statutes, regulations, case precedents, legal texts, and reasoning applied to facts in the particular situation. Over 700 pages of briefs were filed in the United States Supreme Court case of *Miranda v. Arizona*. Though Miranda's lawyers filed a concise brief, many other briefs came to the Court in this case. A number of them were *amicus curiae*, or friends of the court, briefs.[6] These are briefs filed by people who are not parties to the case but who believe they have important comments to make before a ruling is handed down.

Arguments Presented in Court

On Monday, February 2, 1966, Miranda's lawyers and the lawyers for the state of Arizona appeared before the justices of the Supreme Court of the United States for oral arguments. These are arguments for which lawyers actually stand up to make them in person to the justices of the Supreme Court.

Miranda's lawyers had agreed they would base their argument on the Sixth Amendment right to counsel. As the oral arguments proceeded, however, it became clear that the justices were interested in a discussion of the Fifth Amendment privilege against self-incrimination.

When one of the justices asked Flynn, Miranda's lawyer, if the right to a lawyer existed during the interrogation, when the investigation had begun to focus on the accused, Flynn said, "I think that the man at that time has the right to exercise, if he knows, and under the present state of the law in Arizona, if he's rich enough, and if he's educated enough, to assert his Fifth Amendment right, and if he recognizes he has a Fifth Amendment right, to request counsel."

After that comment and several others by Flynn, one of the justices asked if the right to an attorney existed at the time of interrogation, then did every other constitutional right also come into play? Would it then be required that a jury be brought into the interrogation room?

Flynn replied that, certainly, a jury would not be required, that a ruling on Miranda's behalf "would simply extend those constitutional rights which police are about to take away from him." Later in the argument, Flynn would say that Miranda "was called upon to surrender a right that he didn't fully realize and appreciate that he had."

When Flynn was questioned about what a lawyer would advise, if a lawyer were available during questioning, he responded that a lawyer would advise that the accused had the right not to incriminate himself, the right not to make any statement, the right to be free from further questioning by the police department, the right at the ultimate time to be represented adequately by counsel, and that if the accused were too poor to employ counsel, the state would employ counsel for him. Flynn went on to state that the accused had "the right not to be convicted out of his own mouth."

When asked, "Why does the [Fifth] Amendment not protect the rich as well as the poor, the literate as well as the illiterate?" Flynn responded:

I'd say that it [the Fifth Amendment] certainly and most assuredly ... does protect the rich, the educated, the strong, those rich enough to hire counsel, those who are educated enough to know what their rights are, those who are strong enough to withstand police questioning and assert those rights …

At that point, one of the justices said, "I'm asking you only about Fifth Amendment provisions, 'No person shall be compelled to be a witness against himself.' Does that protection [apply] to every person or just some persons … I'm talking about what the Amendment is supposed to do."

Flynn replied, "It is supposed to apply to all persons."

When Flynn's allotted time for oral argument was up, the lawyer for the state of Arizona, Gary Nelson, stood up to offer his oral argument. His position, of course, was that Miranda's conviction should be upheld.

Nelson argued, "The practical effect of introducing counsel at the interrogation stage is going to stop the interrogation for any and all purposes except what counsel decides will be in the best interest of his defendant."

The Court's follow-up question asked then if Nelson thought that if the accused had a lawyer present wouldn't that fulfill the purpose of the Fifth Amendment?

Isn't that about the same thing as the practical effect and object of the Amendment which says 'He shall not be compelled to testify against himself?' Is there any difference between the object, the purposes … what the lawyer tells him and what the Fifth Amendment [provides]? … Isn't that the object of the Amendment?

Nelson's next comment was surprising. It almost sounded as if he were arguing for Miranda.

The pretrial police interrogation does more than just develop confessions; it develops incriminating statements. It develops ... statements which pin a suspect down very closely after the crime has been committed, or very closely after he's been taken into police custody which prevent or ... make it unprofitable for him to perjure himself or change his testimony at the trial.

To that comment, one of the justices asked rhetorically, "Is there anything fantastic in the idea that the Fifth Amendment protection against being compelled to testify against one's self might be read reasonably as meaning there should be no pretrial proceedings when he was there in the possession of the state?"[7]

Deciding the Case

In arriving at its decision in the *Miranda* opinion, the Court looked to the history of confession law as it had evolved in the United States. The opinion discussed, in great detail, the "overzealous police practices" of the past, those practices involving physical brutality.

Specifically, a New York case was mentioned. "[T]he police brutally beat, kicked, and placed lighted cigarette butts on the back of a potential witness under interrogation for the purpose of securing a statement incriminating a third party."

Chief Justice Warren, writing for the majority in his opinion, was clearly outraged at the brutal methods used in the past to coerce confessions. He stated that, though cases of this nature had definitely become the exception, they still existed in sufficient number to be of concern. He believed that something needed to be done to assure that this behavior would be stopped altogether.

The Supreme Court discussed a passage from the Wickersham Report (discussed in chapter 2). The following was included:

Not only does the use of the third degree [unlawful methods of coercing a confession] involve a flagrant violation of law by the officers of the law, but it involves the danger of false confessions, and it tends to make police and prosecutors less zealous in the search for objective evidence. As the New York prosecutor quoted in the report said, "It is a short cut and makes the police lazy and unenterprising." Or as another official quoted remarked: "If you use your fists, you are not so likely to use your wits."

The Court's opinion went on to discuss the fact that the practice of in-custody interrogation had generally become psychologically rather than physically oriented. The Court examined current published guides of police practice. Among them, perhaps, dwelled the strategy used on Ernesto Miranda.

The Supreme Court detailed many tactics recommended in the manuals. The Court discussed the "Mutt and Jeff" strategy (also known as "good cop/bad cop"), where one officer would act friendly and the other would act just the opposite. Another interrogation device examined was the ploy in which officers would advise a suspect that an identification had been made by a number of witnesses when, in fact, no such identification had been made. Privacy was the key element to a successful interrogation, these manuals taught.

Additionally, the manuals referred to in the Supreme Court decision directed that an interrogator's comments should center on *why* the suspect had committed the crime rather than on *whether* the suspect had committed the crime.

In the Supreme Court opinion, the justices detailed specific procedures recommended in police manuals that would appear to deprive the accused of their constitutional rights:

In the event that the subject wishes to speak to a relative or an attorney, the following advice is tendered [given]:

The interrogator should respond by suggesting the subject first tell the truth to the interrogator himself rather than get anyone else involved in the matter. If the request is for an attorney, the interrogator may suggest that the subject save himself or his family the expense of such professional service, particularly if he is innocent of the offense under investigation. The interrogator may also add, "Joe, I'm only looking for the truth, and if you're telling the truth, that's it. You can handle this by yourself."

When normal procedures fail to produce the needed result, the police may resort to deceptive [strategies] such as giving false legal advice. It is important to keep the subject off balance, for example, by trading on his insecurity about himself or his surroundings. The police then persuade, trick, or cajole him out of exercising his constitutional rights ... [8]

Chief Justice Earl Warren, the author of the *Miranda* Supreme Court opinion, was obviously incensed at the methods designed to "trick" suspects into confessing. He stated, "The current practice of incommunicado interrogation is at odds with one of our Nation's most cherished principles—that the individual may not be compelled to incriminate himself."[9]

The Court's Opinion: The Miranda Warning

After discussing confession law at length, the Supreme Court opinion examined the *Escobedo* case and its significance in the *Miranda* ruling.

As might have been predicted, in the *Miranda* decision the Supreme Court decided to expand the *Escobedo* ruling, stating that the Fifth Amendment privilege against self-incrimination was available prior to criminal court proceedings and that a suspect must be told of the right to an attorney. After the *Miranda* decision, "suspects would be afforded the right to counsel in any situation in which freedom of action was curtailed in any significant way."

It is a common belief that the Supreme Court set forth in its decision the specific wording required of the Miranda warning; however, this is not the case. The actual comment in the Supreme Court decision is:

KANSAS CITY, MISSOURI POLICE DEPARTMENT

ADULT MIRANDA WARNING

1. You have the right to remain silent.
2. Anything you say can and will be used against you in a court of law.
3. You have the right to talk to a lawyer and have him present with you while you are being questioned.
4. If you cannot afford to hire a lawyer, one will be appointed to represent you before any questioning, if you wish.
5. You can decide at any time to exercise these rights and not answer any questions or make any statements.

ADULT WAIVER

After the warning and in order to secure a waiver, the following questions should be asked and an affirmative reply secured to each question.

1. Do you understand each of these rights I have explained to you?
2. Having these rights in mind, do you wish to talk to us now?

Law enforcement officers generally carry a card or a sheet of paper like this one with a specific warning to advise suspects of their rights.

Prior to any questioning, the person must be warned that he has a right to remain silent, that any statement he does make may be used as evidence against him, and that he has a right to the presence of an attorney, either retained [hired and paid for by the defendant] or appointed [hired by the court and generally paid by the state].[10]

The Supreme Court opinion went on to state that the defendant could waive or exercise these rights under the *Miranda* ruling at any time prior to or during the questioning. This means that if a defendant has begun to give a statement, but then decides to request an attorney, the questioning must stop immediately and an attorney must be provided.

One practical result of the *Miranda* ruling has been the use of "warning cards" by police. Though the wording of the Miranda warning may vary from state to state, common wording includes:

You have the right to remain silent. Anything you say can and will be used against you in a court of law. You have the right to the presence of an attorney to assist you during questioning, if you so desire. If you cannot afford an attorney, you have the right to have an attorney appointed for you prior to questioning. Do you understand these rights?

When the Supreme Court reversed Miranda's conviction in the kidnap-rape case, Flynn and Frank believed that Miranda's conviction in the robbery case could not be left in place, as the confessions in both cases had been made at the same time, under the same circumstances. This was not to be, as the Supreme Court decided that the *Miranda* ruling was not retroactive. It did not apply to cases decided before the Supreme Court's *Miranda* decision. Lawyers did, however, through complex legal work, later manage to get the original robbery conviction reversed. Even so, Miranda was later retried and convicted on the robbery charge.[11]

Dissenting Opinions

Though the famous Miranda warning came as a result of the United States Supreme Court's opinion in the *Miranda* case, not all Supreme Court justices agreed with the decision. When a Supreme Court opinion is handed down, it becomes law. However, justices in the minority, or those justices who disagree with the majority, have the opportunity to publish dissenting, or disagreeing, opinions. Although these dissenting opinions are published with the majority opinion, they do not become law.

Justice Tom C. Clark, in his dissent, expressed his opinion of the *Miranda* ruling in this way: "Such a strict constitutional specific inserted at the nerve center of crime detection may well kill the patient."[12] Clark, along with other critics, believed that the *Miranda* ruling might well destroy the criminal justice system. In addition, Clark and those with similar beliefs felt that the Supreme Court had gone too far in expanding the rights of the accused while not properly respecting the rights of the victim and of society at large.

Miranda Tried Again: Without the Fruit of the Poisonous Tree

And what happened to Ernesto Miranda after the United States Supreme Court overturned his conviction in the kidnap-rape case? Miranda was ready to celebrate when he heard the news. He believed that he would soon walk out of prison a free man, but this was not to be. Though Miranda's conviction had been reversed, the state of Arizona still had the right to go to trial again on his case in Arizona state court. Ernesto Miranda would have to wait in custody for that trial.[13]

In the second trial, the "fruit of the poisonous tree" would be excluded from evidence, meaning that Miranda's confession could not be heard by the jury. The term "fruit of the poisonous tree" is used to describe a piece of evidence that has come from an illegal procedure. Because the procedure was illegal to begin with, and because the evidence against the defendant may not be used at trial, the evidence is called "fruit of the poisonous tree." Thus, because Miranda's interrogation was illegal, his confession could not be used in court.

John Flynn prepared for Miranda's second trial, which was scheduled to begin on October 24, 1966, but the trial had to be postponed because Rebecca Ann Johnson was pregnant and due to have her baby in November. After Miranda's first trial, Rebecca Ann Johnson had gone about the business of living. She had gotten married and had a child. She was expecting her second.[14]

Finally, on February 15, 1967, almost four years after the crime, Miranda's second trial began. The prosecution had a tough case on its hands. By this time, there were legal questions as to whether Rebecca Ann could identify Ernesto Miranda as the man who had kidnapped and raped her. Miranda's lawyer questioned the validity of Rebecca Ann's identification of Miranda from years before. The lawyer raised many issues regarding her identification of Miranda at the police station, after the lineup. In addition, the jury would not be allowed to hear or see Miranda's confession.

Perhaps Miranda realized what a difficult case this was for the prosecution. He was described as "composed and detached, even slightly amused at times," during the six-hour questioning of possible jurors.[15]

Miranda may have been dismayed, however, at the testimony given by the prosecution's key witness, Twila Hoffman. Hoffman was the mother of Miranda's child and the woman he had been living with at the time he committed Rebecca Ann Johnson's kidnap and rape.

Some reports state that Twila Hoffman came forward to prosecutors and police because Miranda had reported her to welfare authorities and was trying to take their daughter away from her. These same reports state that Miranda had admitted the kidnap-rape to Hoffman during a prison visit and that Miranda had asked Hoffman to offer his hand in marriage to Rebecca Ann Johnson.[16]

Moise Berger, one of the prosecutors in the second *Miranda* trial, went to Hoffman's home. She said, "Come on in." That was their first shock. Berger had thought that Hoffman would be uncooperative. Quite to the contrary, Hoffman was glad to talk about the case.

Hoffman told Berger and Cooley that Miranda had confessed the crime to her while he was in jail. He had told her that he had tied the victim up, taken her to the desert, and raped her.

After a long discussion with Hoffman, Berger asked why she was being so cooperative. As it turned out, while Miranda was in prison, Hoffman and one of her daughters (not Miranda's child) had gone to visit him. After that visit, Berger stated, Hoffman had reason to believe that, if Miranda got out of prison, he would harm Hoffman's daughter.[17]

During the trial, Hoffman testified that not only had Miranda confessed the crime to her, but he had also told her to show Rebecca Ann their infant child. Perhaps seeing the child would encourage Rebecca Ann to drop the charges, he believed.[18]

Miranda Convicted Again

Even without the confession, the jury convicted Miranda on the strength of Twila Hoffman's testimony. Miranda was sentenced to twenty to thirty years in prison.

Miranda was sent to prison, where he was quite popular among the inmates as a result of the famous decision. He appealed, but his conviction was upheld by the Arizona Supreme Court, and then by the United States Supreme Court.

Miranda requested parole on four successive occasions, but it was denied each time. His notoriety might well have been his downfall in repeated bids for freedom.

Ultimately, in December of 1972, Miranda was released on a split vote by the parole board. For the next three years, he was in and out of prison on a variety of charges. He continued to practice his barber trade behind bars.

When Miranda was released in 1975, he was unable to obtain employment as a barber because the law would not allow a barber's license to be issued to a person with his criminal record. Miranda went to work for a tire company. In order to supplement his income, he sold autographed Miranda warning cards for $1.50 to $2.00.[19]

On January 31, 1976, Miranda sat at a table in a bar, gambling in a card game with two other men. "Three dollars!" one of them shouted after an argument broke out.

The barmaid took the cards, and the three men began to fight. Miranda's hands were bloody afterwards, and he went into the restroom to wash.

Before he returned, one of the men who had been involved in the fight passed a large hooked-end folding knife to the other man who had fought with Miranda. "Here, you finish it," he said, and left the bar.

When Miranda came out of the restroom, he scuffled with the man who held the knife. As Miranda tried to wrestle the knife away, the man stabbed him twice, once in the abdomen, once in the chest. Miranda fell to the floor near the pool table. At the age of thirty-five, Ernesto Arturo Miranda was pronounced dead in the emergency room at Good Samaritan Hospital in Phoenix.

When a suspect was arrested in Miranda's murder, the arresting officer pulled out a warning card and began, "You have the right to remain silent … "[20]

Years later, Phoenix citizens would be protected by another officer who carried a Miranda warning card—Ernesto Miranda's nephew. As Justice Robert H. Jackson wisely observed in *Korematsu v. United States*, "If any fundamental assumption underlies our system, it is that guilt is personal and not inheritable."[21]

CHAPTER 6

The Legacy of *Miranda*

When the Supreme Court voted in favor of Miranda, police had to learn the importance of reading the Miranda warning and put it into practice. A confession made during an arrest could only be used in court if a suspect had been read the Miranda rights. This policy is still upheld to this day, but several court decisions have altered its interpretation and some cases weakened it.

The deep division among the Supreme Court justices in this decision mirrored a difference of opinion across the United States. Though many Americans supported the decision, an almost panicky response came from *Miranda*'s critics. A breakdown of law and order was predicted. Many believed that confessions would essentially stop altogether. It was said that the Supreme Court had "handcuffed police" while bending over backwards to safeguard the rights of the "criminal" and ignoring the rights of the victim and the need for society to keep the streets safe.

Not only were critics worried about the predicted drastic decline in confessions and convictions, but they were also concerned about the time and cost of administering the Miranda warning and providing an attorney appointed at taxpayer expense. Critics were ready with the attack.

A Senate judiciary subcommittee called the judge from the second *Miranda* trial to testify regarding the impact of the case on law enforcement in the United States. Senator Sam Ervin called for a constitutional amendment to destroy the effect of the *Miranda* ruling.

Justice John Marshall Harlan, in his dissent to the ruling, predicted "harmful consequences for the country at large." And Duane Nedrud, then Executive Director of the National District Attorneys' Association and one of the "friends of the court" who had filed an *amicus curiae* brief, made a dire prediction, "Fewer crimes will be solved, even fewer crimes will be prosecuted." In addition, almost as a contradiction, Nedrud believed that, ironically, Ernesto Miranda, with an IQ of seventy to seventy-five, would not even have been able to understand his constitutional rights if the Miranda warning had been given to him.[1]

In a setting where this warning was most likely to help those suspects who were poorly educated and uninformed, Nedrud's statement pointed out a true paradox.

Moise Berger, the prosecutor in Miranda's retrial, did not believe that the Miranda ruling helped anyone's rights or liberties. He felt that it was neither good for law enforcement nor the accused. "A lot of people went back on the streets who shouldn't have," he said. And he stated that many cases were thrown out of court because the law was incorrectly applied.

As to protecting the accused, according to Berger, whether or not a suspect talks has little or nothing to do with whether the suspect is told of Miranda rights. Berger cited a particularly brutal case where a man murdered his entire family. Berger was called to the scene by police. He asked a psychiatrist to meet him there. Berger and the psychiatrist spent a great deal of time explaining the suspect's rights to him, giving even more information than is required under the *Miranda* ruling.

Still, the suspect waived his rights and confessed to the murders. When Berger asked the psychiatrist why the suspect had confessed, the psychiatrist replied that the suspect felt guilty about what he had done and wanted to "get it off his chest."[2]

With controversy on many fronts regarding the *Miranda* ruling, the United States Congress in 1976 enacted a law in an attempt to dilute the *Miranda* decision. The law stated that the failure to give the Miranda warning would be only a factor in considering whether a confession was admissible.[3] As a practical matter, this law has not had a great impact on state cases which center on Miranda warning problems.

Stephen Markman, a former assistant attorney general in charge of the United States Office of Legal Policy, was one of the *Miranda* ruling's harshest critics. According to him, many people had begun to stray from a belief that the "principal concern of the justice system should ... be the determination of truth." Instead, Markman said, many people had begun to believe that the justice system should be primarily concerned with a "narrowly defined range" of pseudo civil liberties for defendants. Markman stated in 1987, "Our present difficulties stem from having allowed these ... civil libertarians to stand our Constitution on its head, and their tragic legacy can only be overcome if we put the Constitution back on its feet."[4]

As late as 1986, the twenty-year anniversary of the *Miranda* ruling, United States Attorney General Edwin Meese drew his own conclusions about the case: "I think what *Miranda* did was invent new rights that had never existed before 1966, and I think that the balance of the rights of the respective parties in the criminal justice system was imbalanced then." Meese's conclusions, and earlier predictions by *Miranda* ruling critics, however, did not seem to coincide with the vast majority of research about the actual effect of the decision.[5]

Rights Upheld and Justice Intact

Though many believed that the *Miranda* ruling would cause the criminal justice "sky to fall," this prophecy simply has not come to pass.

On "Nightline," a television news program, Mario Merola, Bronx County (New York) District Attorney, appeared along with then Attorney General Edwin Meese in 1986. Merola's comment was quite the opposite of Meese's. Merola said, "I think that overall that [sic] *Miranda* has not hurt us. We're putting more people away than ever. We have more work than ever. So for us to deal with just a few cases, and you're concerned about that, really I think that *Miranda* is overblown."

Merola believed that the ruling had made police more fair. "There were cases where the individual is beaten and brutalized ... by policemen who were interrogating, and I think that's what *Miranda* has done. It has civilized the whole operation, the criminal justice system and has civilized the police."[6]

As soon as six months after the ruling, Justice Tom C. Clark, one of the dissenting justices in the *Miranda* opinion, said that the decision had not hindered law enforcement as he had expected it might when he wrote his dissenting opinion. After talking to law enforcement officials across the country, Clark discovered that confessions were being made more frequently than before *Miranda*.[7]

Former Chief Justice Warren Burger also stated the view that *Miranda* has not had a negative impact on law enforcement.[8]

And in 1976, United States Attorney General Griffin Bell was quoted as saying, "It [the *Miranda* ruling] protects our rights under the Fifth and Sixth Amendments, and I don't know of any better alternative. It is part of the American way of life now. Even the police don't want to do away with it. And I talked to quite a number of them [while at the Justice Department]."[9]

Though some studies found to the contrary, in 1968 the Institute of Criminal Law and Procedure at Georgetown University found that the percentage of suspects questioned after the *Miranda* ruling dropped only slightly, from 55 to 48 percent.[10]

The anticipated overall drastic decline in confessions following the *Miranda* decision simply never seemed to materialize. Evelle Younger, Los Angeles County District Attorney, made a study

shortly after the ruling in order to determine its impact on law enforcement. What he learned is surprising. Of approximately four thousand felony cases prosecuted in a three-week period within the study, confessions were "essential to a successful prosecution in only a small percentage of criminal cases." Younger's conclusions are interesting. "The most significant things about our findings are that suspects will talk regardless of the warnings, and furthermore, it isn't so all-fired important whether they talk or not."[11]

So, what about the fear that the *Miranda* ruling would be responsible for putting scores of menacing criminals back on the streets? Studies seem to bear out the fact that no such change is taking place. In a 1987 article in the *American Bar Association Journal*, John Kaplan, a law school professor, concluded that suspects offer confessions just as easily with the Miranda warning as without. He concluded that suspects simply feel more inclined to talk when the police are courteous and professional.[12]

Of note is the fact that the *Miranda* ruling made a law of what the FBI had been doing for two decades, informing suspects of their rights. So the type of warnings required by the *Miranda* ruling were certainly nothing new in law enforcement.

And is the *Miranda* case truly worth all the controversy? In July of 1988, a *Newsweek* article reported that fewer than 1 percent of criminal cases had been thrown out because of defective confessions. And of the 1 percent, only a fraction were voided because law enforcement failed to follow *Miranda* guidelines.[13]

Griffin Bell served as the US Attorney General from 1977 to 1979.

Did the doomsday predictions about the burden and expense of administering the Miranda warning come to pass? The burden is certainly not as it was first feared to be. Police officers need only carry a small card or piece of paper and read suspects their rights—certainly no great investment of time.

As for the expense, it was feared that *Miranda* would cause a flood of attorneys to be appointed at the interrogation stage, at taxpayer expense. Again, this fear has proven unfounded.

The *Miranda* ruling does not require that all suspects have an attorney present at the time of incustody interrogation. Rather, the opinion states that suspects have the right to have a lawyer present. An overwhelming majority of suspects continue to give up, or waive, the right. It is important to note here that even if a suspect waives the right to an attorney, any confession given must still be voluntary. In other words, just because a lawyer is not present during questioning, the interrogating officers do not have the right to coerce a confession from a suspect.

Cases That Have Built on *Miranda*

What has happened in the courts since the June 1966 *Miranda* ruling? Have any cases served to overrule this decision?

Though Supreme Court decisions have chipped away at the spirit of the decision, none has served to totally destroy its impact. After many years, the *Miranda* ruling remains intact.

Perhaps one of the earliest and most notable cases to affect the *Miranda* ruling was the 1971 decision, *Harris v. New York*. This case did something no other case had done. It allowed the limited use of a defendant's confession in court, even though the defendant had not been given the Miranda warning. This use, it is critical to point out, however, was limited to impeachment [a demonstration that a witness is less worthy of belief] or contradiction at the time of trial.[14]

The impeachment use comes into play only if the defendant who has given a confession does decide to testify in a criminal case. If, while testifying, the defendant makes comments that contradict statements in the confession he had made earlier, the confession may be used for impeachment purposes. The prosecutor is then allowed to ask the defendant about the contradictory statements in the confession. In this way, the jury actually does have the opportunity to hear the statements made by the defendant in the confession. Impeachment can be a great help in cross-examination, as jurors are less likely to believe the testimony of a witness who has contradicted earlier personal statements.

Before the *Harris* ruling, if the defendant's confession was obtained without a Miranda warning, the confession could not be used for any purpose in court. This has changed since the *Harris* decision was handed down.

The *Harris* impeachment opinion met with great controversy. Those who oppose the *Harris* ruling argue that a confession made without the required warning is "tainted," or bad for all purposes. Those who support the impeachment decision, however, are pleased to see that the Supreme Court has chipped away at the *Miranda* decision. These supporters believe it is only right that if the defendant chooses to take the stand and testify, prosecutors are not forced to sit by while the defendant contradicts prior statements made in a confession.

A More Conservative Supreme Court

When the *Miranda* ruling was established under the Court of Earl Warren, some saw the Supreme Court as liberal. When Republican Richard Nixon was elected president in 1968, he vowed to established a more conservative Supreme Court. Nixon appointed Warren Burger as chief justice and some of its decisions weakened the *Miranda* decision.

In the 1974 case of *Michigan v. Tucker*, police failed to give the complete Miranda warning to the suspect in custody. The suspect was not advised that an attorney would be provided if he could not afford one. Still, the Court upheld the conviction, stating that the other warnings had been given. The Miranda warning are "not themselves rights protected by the Constitution," the Court stated, but are "standards" to "safeguard" or "provide practical reinforcement."[15] The ruling in the *Tucker* case, however, has done little to alter the Miranda warning and the confession cases across the country.

In the *Duckworth v. Eagan* ruling of 1989, the Supreme Court perhaps whittled away a bit more at the *Miranda* decision. In that case, police officers advised the suspect that they were not able to provide an attorney at the time of interrogation. Officers advised the suspect, however, that an attorney would be appointed if and when the suspect went to court.

Surprisingly, in this case, the United States Supreme Court upheld the defendant's conviction, stating that no specific form for the warnings had been set down by the Court. Further, the Court stated that police were not required to provide "on call" lawyers for suspects.[16]

In another case, *North Carolina v. Butler* in 1979, the United States Supreme Court decided that the waiver of rights under the Miranda warning does not have to be in writing.[17] In this setting, perhaps there is a certain question that comes to mind: What's to keep some police officers from simply saying that rights were waived in cases where the Miranda warning were never actually given at all? After all, if oral waivers are acceptable, why not simply testify that the Miranda rights had been waived orally?

Initially, it must be understood that many ethical police officers protect citizens across the country. These ethical officers would not engage in this type of activity. A further safeguard, however, is provided in the law. In order to appreciate this safeguard, it is important to examine what actually happens in court. Any time a witness testifies, credibility is an important issue. Jurors may believe all, some, or none of what a witness says. This policy encourages police officers to get a Miranda waiver in writing rather than face a court challenge later regarding whether a waiver was made orally.

Continuing Challenges to *Miranda*

The *United States v. Garibay* added a twist to *Miranda* in 1998. Jose Rosario Garibay, who appealed a violation related to importing marijuana, barely spoke English and clearly showed a lack of understanding. Law officers said that Garibay had waived his rights when arrested, but the Court ruled that the waiver was not valid because Garibay had a low IQ and poor English skills. The case established a precedent that the rights must be translated.[18]

One of the biggest challenges to *Miranda* came in 2000 with the case *Dickerson v. United States.* A lawyer opposed to the *Miranda* decision found a largely ignored law had passed that would have allowed confessions elicited without a police advisory to be used at trial so long as it was demonstrated that they were given voluntarily. If the lawyers won this case, police would no longer have to read the Miranda warning. The Supreme Court, however, overwhelmingly upheld *Miranda* ruling by a vote of 7-2. Defending *Miranda*, Chief Justice William Rehnquist said, "*Miranda* has become embedded in routine police practice to the point where the warnings have become part of our national culture."[19]

In 2004, Miranda again faced a challenge with the case *Missouri v. Seibert.* The case was about police who arrested a woman and elicited a confession, and then advised her of her rights. Her lawyers said that her statements about her involvement in a murder plot were inadmissible because she gave them before her rights were read. The Supreme Court again defended *Miranda* and halted this practice.[20]

In 2010, the justices handed down a decision in a case called *Berghuis v. Thompkins* that further analyzed Miranda rights. In this case, Van Chester Thompkins was questioned about fatally shooting a person in Southfield, Michigan. Thompkins was read his rights before questioning, and he was asked to read one of the rights aloud to prove he understood. He would not, however, sign a form indicating that he understood his rights. At one point while being questioned, he asked God to forgive him for the shooting. He made a motion to stop this evidence from being submitted in court because he said he did not waive his rights. In a close 5-4 decision, the justices decided he had waived his right to remain silent when he knowingly and voluntarily made a statement to police.[21]

Looking at the Miranda warning and the possible waiver of Miranda rights, it is logical to wonder what actually happens in court when a defendant challenges the admissibility of a confession. In order to make such a challenge, the lawyers must discuss the fact that a confession exists. And generally, the defendant takes the stand to testify about how the confession was obtained and whether warnings were given. But what about the Fifth Amendment privilege against self-incrimination? If the defendant does not want to testify but does want to raise a legal issue regarding the confession, what keeps the jury from hearing what the defendant and the lawyers have to say?

The defendant is entitled to a hearing, which is a private discussion by lawyers and the judge in consideration of a point of law. This hearing, held outside the presence of a jury, is for the sole purpose of determining whether the confession is admissible. Thus, if a defendant wants to challenge the admissibility of the confession but does not want the jury to even know that a confession exists, the defendant may testify without the jury in the courtroom. If the judge rules that the confession is not admissible and the defendant chooses not to testify, the jury hears nothing about a confession at all.

Even with the United States Supreme Court modifications of the *Miranda* decision, the Court appears to have no intention of overruling its opinion.

Does the *Miranda* Ruling Apply to Other Evidence?

What about evidence other than the defendant's confession that might be brought into court?

Suppose a suspect is taken to the hospital and blood is drawn while the suspect is unconscious. What happens if, as a result of the blood test, the suspect is charged with driving while intoxicated or driving while under the influence of drugs? Can the prosecutor inform the jury that the defendant's blood test revealed intoxication? The blood test would indeed tend to show the defendant's guilt. Is there a privilege against self-incrimination in this setting under the *Miranda* ruling? Would the police and prosecutors need a Miranda waiver from the defendant in order to bring blood test results to the jury?

No, because the rights under the *Miranda* ruling do not extend to protection from physical evidence, such as a blood test. These rights extend only to statements made by the suspect, as *Schmerber v. California* clarified.[22]

In deciding *Miranda* type cases, the Supreme Court is precariously perched on a tightrope. The Court is flexible in its

The *Miranda* case changed the way police interacted with suspects.

ability to apply the law to a variety of fact situations. This is well illustrated by the cases that have followed the *Miranda* ruling.

As justices retire from the United States Supreme Court and the president appoints new justices to fill the vacancies, the application of the *Miranda* ruling and other cases will most certainly be affected. The varying composition of the Supreme Court has a profound impact on the criminal justice system.

The initial outcry over the effect of the *Miranda* ruling has died down considerably, though some critics remain vocal. Balancing the rights of the defendant with the rights of society and the victim has never been an easy task. As a famous legal scholar once said, "It is better that ten guilty persons escape than that one innocent suffer."[23] This is one of the cornerstones upon which the United States criminal justice system has been built.

Undoubtedly, it can be difficult to determine who has actually committed a crime. Perhaps all signs point to guilt; however, the suspect may truly be innocent. In the United States, the accused is presumed innocent unless proven guilty beyond a reasonable doubt. Throughout the ages, bizarre twists and turns in criminal cases have shocked the public. Just when assumptions have been made and guilt seems obvious, a piece of evidence may surprise everyone. The right to have a criminal case heard in court, in order that evidence may be introduced and weighed, is a fundamental right of all Americans.

And this right is exercised in courtrooms across the country every day. When Miranda warning questions come into play in these courtrooms, a criminal justice system steeped in years of tradition and legal precedent goes into action to uncover evidence and produce results. And these results come about with the understanding that the *Miranda* ruling is alive and well.

It is likely that the *Miranda* ruling will continue in force for many years to come, perhaps for the entire future of the United States criminal justice system. Thus, when future suspects are taken into custody, among the first words from the arresting officer will be,

You have the right to remain silent.

Questions to Consider

1. You are the lawyer for a person who is accused of burglary. You learn that your client, the accused, was not told that she had the right to remain silent. She was, however, told that she had the right to an attorney and that if she could not afford an attorney, one would be appointed to represent her. Your client signed a confession in which she waived her right to have an attorney present. What is your argument to the court regarding this confession?

2. You are the lawyer for a person who is accused of assault. The accused's primary language is Spanish, and he speaks very little English. The police officers explain that when the accused was arrested, he was given his Miranda warning, then asked if he understood the warning. He nodded his head in the affirmative and replied, "Yes." After the police took the accused into an interrogation room at the police station, they had difficulty understanding him and asked that an interpreter come to translate. The interpreter did not give the Miranda warning to the accused in Spanish. During the questioning, the accused

admitted having participated in the commission of a crime. What arguments would you make as the accused's attorney? What do you think the attorney for the state would have to say? How do you think the judge would rule?

3. Some say that people like Ernesto Miranda who are not well educated do not understand the Miranda warning when they are given it. What, then, is the purpose of the warnings? Should a new Supreme Court ruling come down to discontinue the warnings? Why? Why not?

4. Some political commentators have stated that the controversy over the *Miranda* ruling is overblown. They believe that whether or not a suspect gives a confession is of relatively little importance. What are the arguments that support this position?

5. The year is 1965. You have been appointed by the court to represent an indigent defendant. She was taken from the scene of a murder to the police station for questioning. She did not have a lawyer of her own, and she was not told that she had the right to have an attorney present at the time of questioning. Your client, of her own free will, without coercion, gave a confession to the police. The confession described the crime in detail. When the case was tried in the state court, you tried to keep the jury from hearing the confession. The judge allowed the confession to be heard, and your client was convicted. You and your client appealed the case to the state supreme court, where the conviction was upheld. Now the case has been appealed to the United States Supreme Court. Will you base your argument on the Fifth Amendment or the Sixth Amendment? Why?

6. You represent a defendant who was properly given his Miranda warning after arrest, before questioning. He waived those

rights and began to give the police a statement. After several minutes, your client reconsidered. He said that he did not wish to continue his confession and that he would like to have a lawyer. The police officers immediately stopped the questioning and requested that an attorney be provided. While your client sat in the interrogation room waiting for a lawyer, he began to feel uncomfortable and decided that he should "come clean" and give the details of the crime he had committed. Before the lawyer arrived, he blurted out details of the crime to the police. What is your position regarding your client's confession? Why?

7. Comments are often made in the media regarding the "technicalities" of the law. Was Ernesto Miranda's case decided on a technicality? Should the law be changed so that cases cannot be decided on technicalities? Why? Why not?

8. A defendant was convicted of murder and sentenced to death. The murder was particularly brutal and left the victim's family in a shambles, both emotionally and financially. The defendant's conviction was based primarily on a confession given by the defendant without Miranda warning. Now the defendant's conviction has been reversed. The United States Supreme Court has ruled that the confession may not be used in a future trial. The prosecution has insufficient evidence to convict without the confession, so the defendant will go free. Has there been an abuse of justice? Is it wrong that the defendant will be free as the result of a failure to give the Miranda warning? Does this case give enough reason for the Supreme Court to reverse its ruling in the *Miranda* case? If so, how far should the Supreme Court go in removing rights from the accused?

9. You are in law school, and you are very enthusiastic about practicing criminal defense law when you graduate. You will

be defending a variety of clients, some of them like Ernesto Miranda. Your clients may sometimes admit to you that they have committed the crimes with which they are charged. You are approached by your sister and grandmother, both of whom have been victims of violent crimes. They are horrified by your choice and cannot imagine how you could possibly consider a career in which you would be defending "those murderers, baby abusers, and rapists." They want to know how you could set criminals free to roam the streets and commit crimes again. What do you tell them?

10. Those who support the *Miranda* decision and the line of confession cases leading up to it state that stricter laws regarding confessions require that police officers work harder. Without confessions, these supporters contend, officers must get out and work to find leads and hard evidence. In the second Ernesto Miranda trial, the state of Arizona introduced evidence from Twila Hoffman. Indeed, officers and prosecutors did not even learn about the information Hoffman had to offer until weeks before the second trial. Does this fact support the position that some officers may not work as hard to get information about a case if they can get a confession from the suspect? Why? Why not?

Primary Source Documents

Excerpts from the *Miranda v. Arizona* Decision

At the outset, if a person in custody is to be subjected to interrogation, he must first be informed in clear and unequivocal terms that he has the right to remain silent. For those unaware of the privilege, the warning is needed simply to make them aware of it—the threshold requirement for an intelligent decision as to its exercise. More important, such a warning is an absolute prerequisite in overcoming the inherent pressures of the interrogation atmosphere. It is not just the subnormal or woefully ignorant who succumb to an interrogator's imprecations, whether implied or expressly stated, that the interrogation will continue until a confession is obtained or that silence in the face of accusation is itself damning and will bode ill when presented to a jury. Further, the warning will show the individual that his interrogators are prepared to recognize his privilege should he choose to exercise it. ...

The warning of the right to remain silent must be accompanied by the explanation that anything said can and will be used against the individual in court. This warning is needed in order to make him aware not only of the privilege, but also of the consequences of forgoing it. It is only through an awareness of these consequences that there can be any assurance of real understanding and intelligent exercise of the privilege. Moreover, this warning may serve to make the individual more acutely aware that he is faced with a phase of the adversary system—that he is not in the presence of persons acting solely in his interest.

The ... right to have counsel present at the interrogation is indispensable to the protection of the Fifth Amendment privilege under the system we delineate today. ... Thus, the need for counsel to protect the Fifth Amendment privilege comprehends not merely a right to consult with counsel prior to questioning, but also to have counsel present during any questioning if the defendant so desires. ...

An individual need not make a pre-interrogation request for a lawyer. While such request affirmatively secures his right to have one, his failure to ask for a lawyer does not constitute a waiver. No effective waiver of the right to counsel during interrogation can be recognized unless specifically made after the warnings we here delineate have been given. The accused who does not know his rights and therefore does not make a request may be the person who most needs counsel. ...

Accordingly we hold that an individual held for interrogation must be clearly informed that he has the right to consult with a lawyer and to have the lawyer with him during interrogation under the system for protecting the privilege we delineate today. ...

If an individual indicates that he wishes the assistance of counsel before any interrogation occurs, the authorities cannot rationally ignore or deny his request on the basis that the individual does not have or cannot afford a retained attorney. The financial ability of the individual has no relationship to the scope of the rights involved here. The privilege against self-incrimination secured by the Constitution applies to all individuals. The need for counsel in order to protect the privilege exists for the indigent as well as the affluent. ...

In order fully to apprise a person interrogated of the extent of his rights under this system then, it is necessary to warn him not only that he has the right to consult with an attorney, but also that if he is indigent a lawyer will be appointed to represent him. Without this additional warning, the admonition of the right to consult with counsel would often be understood as meaning only that he can consult with a lawyer if he has one or has the funds to obtain one. The warning of a right to counsel would be hollow if not couched in terms that would convey to the indigent—the person most often subjected to interrogation—the knowledge that he too has a right to have counsel present. ...

To summarize, we hold that when an individual is taken into custody or otherwise deprived of his freedom by the authorities in any significant way and is subjected to questioning, the privilege against self-incrimination is jeopardized. Procedural safeguards must be employed to protect the privilege, and unless other fully effective means are adopted to notify the person of his right of silence and to assure that the exercise of the right will be scrupulously honored, the following measures are required. He must be warned prior to any questioning that he has the right to remain silent, that anything he says can be used against him in a court of law, that he has the right to the presence of an attorney, and that if he cannot afford an attorney one will be appointed for him prior to any questioning if he so desires. Opportunity to exercise these rights must be afforded to him throughout the interrogation. After such warnings have been given, and such opportunity afforded him, the individual may knowingly and intelligently waive these rights and agree to answer questions or make a statement. But unless and until such warnings and waiver are demonstrated by the prosecution at trial, no evidence obtained as a result of interrogation can be used against him.

Chronology

December 15, 1791 The Bill of Rights is ratified, adding the Fifth and Sixth Amendments. The Fifth Amendment protects an individual from being pressured to be a witness against himself or herself in a criminal case. The Sixth Amendment guarantees a group of rights for criminal defendants, including the right to a speedy and public trial, the right to a lawyer, the right to an impartial jury, the right to know your accusers and the nature of the evidence and charges against you.

July 28, 1868 The Fourteenth Amendment is added to the US Constitution, granting citizenship to "all persons born or naturalized in the United States," including former slaves who had been recently freed after the Civil War. It also it forbids any state to deny any person "life, liberty or property, without due process of law"—a key point in the *Miranda* case.

March 3, 1963 Ernesto Miranda, age twenty-three, abducts and rapes an eighteen-year-old woman in Phoenix who is on her way home from work.

March 13, 1963 Miranda is arrested and interrogated by police. He confesses to the crime, but he is not told of his right to have a lawyer before questioning.

March 18, 1963 The US Supreme Court rules in *Gideon v. Wainwright* that, according to the Fourteenth Amendment, states are required to provide legal counsel to criminal defendants who cannot afford to pay for their own lawyer.

June 27, 1963 Ernesto Miranda is convicted and sentenced to two concurrent terms of twenty to thirty years in prison.

August 1963 Alvin Moore, Miranda's lawyer, appeals his case to the Arizona State Supreme Court. The court finds that Miranda's constitutional rights were not violated because he did not specifically request a lawyer.

June 22, 1964 The US Supreme Court decides in *Escobedo v. Illinois* that criminal suspects have a right to a lawyer during police questioning under the Sixth Amendment.

April 1965 The Arizona State Supreme Court rejects an appeal by Miranda to hear his case again, and the conviction is upheld.

June 1965 Miranda's lawyers submit a request to the US Supreme Court to review his case, arguing that his Fifth Amendment rights had been violated.

November 1965 The Supreme Court agrees to hear Miranda's case.

February–March 1966 The Supreme Court hears the oral arguments in *Miranda v. Arizona*.

June 13, 1966 The Supreme Court rules in favor of Miranda, finding that detained criminal suspects, before being questioned by police, must be told of their constitutional right to a lawyer and against self-incrimination.

Summer 1966 A popular version of the Miranda warning is written and distributed to police across the US.

February 15–March 1, 1967 Ernesto Miranda is again put on trial for rape and convicted for a second time.

June 10, 1974 The US Supreme Court rules in *Michigan v. Tucker* that Miranda rights are "not themselves rights protected by the Constitution" but are "standards" meant to protect rights.

January 31, 1976 Ernesto Miranda dies in a bar room brawl. His accused attacker is read the Miranda warning when arrested.

June 25, 2000 The US Supreme Court in *Dickerson v. United States* upholds the requirement that the Miranda warning be read to criminal suspects and struck down a federal statute that claimed to overrule *Miranda v. Arizona*.

June 1, 2010 The US Supreme Court in *Berghuis v. Thompkins* finds that the mere act of remaining silent is not enough to imply that a suspect has invoked his or her Miranda rights.

Chapter Notes

Chapter 1. Rights for the Accused

1. Richard C. Cortner and Clifford M. Lytle, *Constitutional Law and Politics: Three Arizona Case Studies* (Tucson, AZ: The University of Arizona Press, 1971), p. 9.

2. As reported in the departmental records of the Phoenix (Arizona) Police Department.

3. Ibid.; Trial transcripts of Miranda's first trial, as included in Petitioner's Brief to the United States Supreme Court, RG 267, National Archives, pp. 22–23, 34–35.

4. As reported in the departmental records of the Phoenix (Arizona) Police Department.

5. Ibid.

6. Lisa Baker, *Miranda: Crime, Law, and Politics* (New York, NY: Atheneum, 1983), p. 12.

Chapter 2.   History Leading Up to the Landmark Case

1. Peter Baird, "Miranda Memories," *Litigation*, Winter 1990, p. 43; Herbert M. Atherton, ed., *1791–1991: The Bill of Rights and Beyond* (undated), pp. 41–42.

2. Lisa Baker, *Miranda: Crime, Law and Politics* (New York, NY: Atheneum, 1983), p. 67.

3. *Miranda v. Arizona*, 384 U.S. 436 (1966).

4. Kermit L. Hall, *The Oxford Companion to the Supreme Court of the United States* (New York, NY: Oxford University Press: 1992), pp. 661–662; *Powell v. Alabama*, 287 U.S. 45 (1932).

5. *Brown v. Mississippi*, 297 U.S. 278 (1936).

6. Hall, p. 96; *Brown v. Mississippi*, 297 U.S. 278 (1936).

7. Hall, pp. 552–553; Gary Chamberlain, "Crime, Confessions, and the Supreme Court," *America*, July 8, 1967, pp. 32–33.

8. Ibid.

9. Ibid., p. 33.

10. Hall, pp. 338–339; *Gideon v. Wainwright*, 372 U.S. 335 (1963).

11. *Argersinger v. Hamlin*, 407 U.S. 103 (1972).

12. Baker, p. 76.

13. Hall, pp. 518–519; *Malloy v. Hogan*, 378 U.S. 1 (1964).

14. Andrew David, *Famous Supreme Court Cases* (Minneapolis, MN: Lerner Publications, 1980), pp. 76–78; *Escobedo v. Illinois*, 378 U.S. 478(1964).

15. Baker, pp. 26–28.

16. As reported in departmental reports of the Phoenix (Arizona) Police Department; Trial transcripts of Miranda's first trial, as included in Petitioner's Brief to the United States Supreme Court, RG 267, National Archives.

Chapter 3. Making a Case for Miranda

1. As reported in departmental records of the Phoenix (Arizona) Police Department.

2. Reports from psychiatrists James A. Kilgore and Leo Rubinow; Peter Baird, "Miranda Memories," *Litigation*, Winter 1990, p. 43; and Herbert M. Atherton, ed., *1791–1991: The Bill of Rights and Beyond* (undated), pp. 9–12.

3. Ibid., p. 12.

4. As reported in the departmental reports of the Phoenix (Arizona) Police Department.

5. Lisa Baker, *Miranda: Crime, Law and Politics* (New York, NY: Atheneum, 1983), pp. 9–12.

6. As reported in the departmental reports of the Phoenix (Arizona) Police Department; Trial transcripts of Miranda's first trial, as included in the Petitioner's Brief to the United States Supreme Court, RG 267, National Archives, pp. 40–41.

7. Baird, p. 44.

8. As reported in the psychiatric reports of James M. Kilgore and Leo Rubinow.

9. Trial transcripts of Miranda's first trial, as included in the Petitioner's Brief to the United States Supreme Court, RG 267, National Archives, p. 55.

10. Ibid., p. 41.

11. Ibid., pp. 36–45; Respondent's Brief filed in the United States Supreme Court, RG 267, National Archives, p. 19.

12. Baker, p. 13.

13. Trial transcripts of Miranda's first trial, as included in Petitioner's Brief to the United States Supreme Court, RG 267, National Archives, p. 41.

14. Baird, p. 45.

15. *Miranda v. Arizona*, 98 Ariz. 18 (1965).

16. Baker, pp. 62–63; Peter Baird, "The Confessions of Ernesto Arturo Miranda," *Arizona Attorney*, October 1991, p. 22.

17. Richard C. Cortner and Clifford M. Lytle, *Constitutional Law and Politics: Three Arizona Case Studies* (Tucson, AZ: The University of Arizona Press, 1971), p. 22; Baird, "Confessions," p. 23.

18. Baker, p. 83.

19. Petitioner's Brief to the United States Supreme Court, RG 267, National Archives, p. 49.

Chapter 4. Arizona's Argument Against Miranda

1. From notation on the prosecutor's copy of departmental reports of the Phoenix (Arizona) Police Department.

2. Ibid.

3. Judgment and Sentence, RG 107 Maricopa County, SG 8 Superior Court, Arizona State Archives, Department of Library, Archives and Public Records, Phoenix, AZ.

4. Trial transcripts of Miranda's first trial as included in Petitioner's Brief to the United States Supreme Court, RG 267, National Archives.

5. Lisa Baker, *Miranda: Crime, Law and Politics* (New York, NY: Atheneum, 1983), p. 22.

6. Trial transcripts of Miranda's first trial as included in Petitioner's Brief to the United States Supreme Court, RG 267, National Archives.

7. Ibid., pp. 62–67.

8. Richard C. Cortner and Clifford M. Lytle, *Constitutional Law and Politics: Three Arizona Case Studies* (Tucson, AZ: The University of Arizona Press, 1971), p. 19.

9. *Miranda v. Arizona*, 98 Ariz. 18 (1965).

10. Peter Baird, "The Confessions of Ernesto Arturo Miranda," *Arizona Attorney*, October 1991, pp. 22–23.

11. Baker, p. 84.

12. Petitioner's Brief to the United States Supreme Court, RG 267, National Archives; Audiotapes of the Oral Arguments in the United States Supreme Court, Records of the Supreme Court of the United States, RG 267.575 and RG 267.576, National Archives.

13. Petitioner's Brief to the United States Supreme Court, RG 267, National Archives.

Chapter 5. The Supreme Court Rules

1. Peter Baird, "Miranda Memories," *Litigation*, Winter 1990, p. 45.

2. Liz Sonneborn, *Supreme Court Cases Through Primary Sources: Miranda v. Arizona* (New York, NY: Rosen, 2004), p. 34.

3. Lisa Baker, *Miranda: Crime, Law and Politics* (New York, NY: Atheneum, 1983), pp. 60–61.

4. Ibid., p. 63.

5. Ibid., pp. 87–88.

6. Ibid., p. 110.

7. Audiotapes of the Oral Arguments in the United States Supreme Court, Records of the Supreme Court of the United States, RG 267.575 and RG 267.576, National Archives.

8. *Miranda v. Arizona*, 384 U.S. 436 (1966).

9. Ibid.

10. Ibid.

11. Peter Baird, "The Confessions of Ernesto Arturo Miranda," *Arizona Attorney*, October 1991, pp. 24–25.

12. Dissent to *Miranda v. Arizona*, 384 U.S. 436 (1966).

13. Baker, p. 191.

14. Ibid., p. 192; "Rapist Asked, 'Pray for Me,' Jury Is Told," *Arizona Republic*, February 17, 1967.

15. "Jury Picked for Retrial of Miranda," *Arizona Republic*, February 16, 1967.

16. Baker, p. 192.

17. Moise Berger, telephone conversation with author, July 30, 1993.

18. Trial transcripts, Ernesto Miranda retrial, RG 107 Maricopa County, SG 8 Superior Court, Arizona State Archives, Department of Library, Archives and Public Records, Phoenix, AZ.

19. "Second Rape Conviction for Miranda," *Arizona Republic*, February 25, 1967.

20. Baird, "Confessions," p. 25.

21. *Korematsu v. United States*, 323 U.S. 214 (1944).

Chapter 6. The Legacy of *Miranda*

1. Gary Chamberlain, "Crime, Confessions and the Supreme Court," *America*, July 8, 1967, pp. 32–33.

2. Moise Berger, telephone conversation with author, July 30, 1993.

3. Discussion of U.S.C. 3501, in Ronald Colins, Thomas S. Schrock, and Robert C. Welsh, "Interrogational Rights: Reflections on *Miranda v. Arizona*," *Southern California Law Review* 52, 1978–79.

4. Jonathon I. Z. Agronsky, "Meese v. Miranda: The Final Countdown," *American Bar Association Journal*, November 1, 1987, p. 87.

5. "Miranda Ruling," ABC Nightline, June 13, 1986.

6. Ibid.

7. Chamberlain, p. 33; Tom C. Clark, "Gideon Revisited," 15 *Arizona Law Review* 343 (1973).

8. Peter Baird, "Critics Must Confess, *Miranda* was the Right Decision," *The Wall Street Journal*, June 13, 1991.

9. Agronsky, pp. 88–89.

10. "Miranda Decision Study Shows Weakness in Enforcement," *Arizona Republic*, May 14, 1986.

11. Chamberlain, p. 34.

12. Agronsky, pp. 88–89.

13. Baird, "Critics Must Confess;" "Fighting Crime by the Rules," *Newsweek*, July 18, 1988, p. 53.

14. *Harris v. New York*, 401 U.S. 222 (1971).

15. *Michigan v. Tucker*, 417 U.S. 433 (1974).

16. *Duckworth v. Eagan*, 492 U.S. 195 (1989).

17. *North Carolina v. Butler*, 441 U.S. 369 (1979).

18. "*United States v. Garibay*," FindLaw, caselaw.findlaw.com/us-9th-circuit/1396556.html.

19. Liz Sonneborn, *Supreme Court Cases Through Primary Sources: Miranda v. Arizona* (New York, NY: Rosen, 2004), p. 34.

20. *Missouri v. Seibert*, Cornell University Law School, www.law.cornell.edu/supct/html/02-1371.ZO.html.

21. *Berghuis v. Thompkins*, Oyez, www.oyez.org/cases/2009/08-1470.

22. *Schmerber v. California*, 384 U.S. 757 (1966).

23. Sir William Blackstone, *Commentaries on the Laws of England,* 1765–1769.

Glossary

admissibility Whether or not information about a case will be allowed to be heard in court. The judge rules on the admissibility of the evidence.

amicus curiae A brief filed by someone who is not a party to the case, but who has an interest in the law that will be made as a result of the decision. "Amicus curiae" is a Latin term meaning "friend of the court."

brief A document filed by lawyers in support of an issue, or issues, of law.

burden of proof The test that the prosecutor or plaintiff must meet in order to win the case. In a criminal case, the burden, beyond a reasonable doubt, is much more difficult to meet than the burden in a civil case, by a preponderance of the evidence.

case or controversy A legal concept providing that justices, and other federal judges, may rule only if an actual dispute is brought before them. Though justices have the power to make law, they cannot make law regarding an issue that is not involved in a case that they are reviewing.

complaining witness The victim in a criminal case.

counsel The lawyer or lawyers conducting the case.

credibility The believability of, or weight to be given to, a witness's testimony. The jurors (or judge when there is no jury) may believe all, some, or none of what a witness has to say.

defendant's failure to testify In a criminal case, the defendant is under no legal obligation to testify. If the defendant chooses not to testify, the judge and the jury are not permitted to consider this failure to testify for any purpose.

defense attorney The lawyer who represents the accused in a criminal case.

dissenting opinion A disagreeing opinion to a court ruling. The written court ruling becomes law. The dissent does not.

due process A legal concept consisting of many legal guarantees and providing that a person accused of a crime will be treated fairly. Due process is a safeguard against cruel or arbitrary procedures.

evidence Information brought into court regarding a case. Evidence may consist of testimony, documents, and physical evidence, such as guns, knives, and other objects that are important to the case.

fruit of the poisonous tree A legal concept providing that if evidence has been obtained illegally, it may not be used in court.

grounds The legal reason for a lawyer's objection.

hearing A discussion by the judge and lawyers regarding a matter of law. The jury is not allowed to hear the discussion.

impeachment The process by which a witness's testimony is attacked. The witness may generally be discredited through prior inconsistent statements.

indigent A defendant who is unable to pay for legal representation.

interrogation The questioning of a witness or suspect by law enforcement officers.

lineup The placing of a suspect with a group of people who are viewed by the victim or another witness to a crime. A lineup is supposed to include people of similar appearance. Generally, the suspect cannot see the victim/witness viewing the lineup. The lineup is sometimes called a "showup."

majority opinion The decision agreed upon by the majority of the justices. The majority opinion is written and becomes law.

oral argument The arguments made in person by parties to a case, and others with a legitimate interest in the case, before members of the court. Lawyers usually make a statement first, and then respond to questions asked by justices.

pauper's form A document that must be filed with a petition for writ of certiorari if the defendant is indigent (unable to pay required fees for an appeal to the United States Supreme Court.)

precedent A case or the body of law made up of prior decisions on the same or similar legal questions.

pro bono A lawyer's acceptance of a case without charging a fee.

prosecutor An official, also known as a district attorney, who represents the state in criminal proceedings.

statute A law.

testimony The information given in court by witnesses in response to questions.

writ of certiorari A document to request that the United States Supreme Court hear a case.

Further Reading

Books

Black, Ryan C. and Ryan J. Owens. *U.S. Supreme Court Decisions and Their Audiences*. Cambridge: Cambridge University Press, 2016.

Daley James. *Landmark Decisions of the U.S. Supreme Court*. North Chelmsford, MA: Courier Corporation, 2012.

McCloskey, Robert and Sanford Levinson. *The American Supreme Court, Sixth Edition*. Chicago, IL: University of Chicago Press, 2016.

Stuart, Gary. *Miranda: The Story of America's Right to Remain Silent*. Tuscon, AZ: University of Arizona Press, 2013.

Vander Hook, Sue. *Miranda v. Arizona: An Individual's Rights When Under Arrest*. Minneapolis, MN: ABDO Publishing Company, 2012.

Websites

Supreme Court of the United States

www.supremecourt.gov/

The site features opinions, oral arguments, and case documents.

MirandaRights.org

www.mirandarights.org/

Information dedicated to helping people understand their Miranda rights.

Landmark Cases of the US Supreme Court

www.landmarkcases.org/en/landmark/home

A resource featuring all the landmark cases of the Supreme Court.

Index

A

admissibility, 42, 95

American Bar Association Journal, 89

American Civil Liberties Union (ACLU), 43

amicus curiae (friend of the court), 49, 68, 84

appeal, 20, 27, 32, 35, 42, 43, 44, 45, 46, 55, 56, 57, 58, 61, 64, 65, 67, 80, 93

Arizona State Industrial School for Boys, 36

Arizona State prison farm, 42

Arizona Supreme Court, 42, 43, 46, 56, 57, 65, 66, 80

assailant, 7, 8

B

Bell, Griffin, 87

Berger, Moise, 79, 80, 84, 85

Berghuis v. Thompkins, 94

"beyond a reasonable doubt," 52, 54, 98

"beyond a shadow of a doubt," 52, 53

Bill of Rights, 13, 14

Black, Hugo L., 24, 44

brief, 46, 47, 48, 49, 60, 61, 67, 68, 84

Brown, Ed, 21, 22

Brown v. Mississippi, 21, 22, 23, 25, 33, 34, 47

burden of proof, 52

Burger, Warren, 87, 92

C

case or controversy, 64

certiorari, 65, 66, 67

civil rights, 33

Civil War, 15

Clark, Tom, 77, 87

confession law, 25, 71, 74

constitutional rights, 15, 25, 29, 32, 34, 37, 43, 57, 60, 67, 69, 73, 74, 84

Cooley, Carroll F., 37, 41, 48, 50, 51, 80

Corcoran, Robert, 43, 44

credibility, 93

D

defendant's failure to testify, 14

Dickerson v. United States, 94

DiGerlando, Benedict, 30, 32

dissenting opinion, 77, 87

Douglas, William O., 24

Duckworth v. Eagan, 92

due process, 15, 18, 20, 47, 63

E

Ellington, Yank, 21, 22

Ervin, Sam, 84

Escobedo, Danny, 30, 32, 58, 60

Escobedo v. Illinois, 30, 33, 34, 41, 43, 46, 48, 57, 58, 67, 74

evidence, 5, 14, 23, 40, 42, 47, 52, 53, 54, 72, 76, 78, 95, 96, 98

F

Federal Bureau of Investigation (FBI), 65, 89

federal laws, 16

Fifth Amendment, 14, 16, 17, 23, 29, 44, 45, 46, 68, 69, 70, 71, 74, 87, 95

Flynn, John, 44, 47, 48, 57, 58, 61, 66, 68, 69, 70, 76, 78

Fourteenth Amendment, 15, 18, 20, 22, 23, 24, 27, 29, 32, 47, 56

Frank, John, 44, 45, 47, 48, 57, 58, 61, 66, 76

fruit of the poisonous tree, 78

G

Garibay, Jose Rosario, 93, 94

Garibay case, see *United States v. Garibay*

Georgetown University, 87

Gideon, Clarence Earl, 27

Gideon v. Wainwright, 25, 27, 29, 30, 32, 33, 34, 46, 47

"good cop/bad cop," see "Mutt and Jeff" strategy

Good Samaritan Hospital, 81

H

"hands-off" doctrine, 18

Harlan, John Marshall, 84

Harris v. New York, 90, 91

hearing, 29, 52, 58, 95

Hoffman, Twila, 36, 79, 80

I

impeachment, 91

indigent, 27, 47

Institute of Criminal Law and Procedure, see Georgetown University interrogation, 10, 15, 27, 28, 30, 32, 37, 39, 41, 43, 44, 46, 47, 48, 49, 58, 65, 68, 69, 70, 71, 72, 73, 74, 78, 90, 92

J

Johnson, Rebecca Ann, 7, 12, 35, 36, 37, 38, 39, 50, 55, 56, 61, 78, 79

K

Kaplan, John, 89
Korematsu v. United States, 82

L

legal representation, 25, 40
Lewis, Roca, Scoville, Beauchamps & Linton, 44
Lilburne, John, 14, 15
lineup, 10, 37, 38, 46, 51, 60, 79

M

majority opinion, 77
Malloy, William, 29
Malloy v. Hogan, 29, 30, 33, 34
Maricopa County Attorney's Office, 49
Markman, Stephen, 85, 86
Meese, Edwin, 86
Merola, Mario, 86, 87
Michigan v. Tucker, 92
Miranda rights, see Miranda warning
Miranda waiver, 93, 96

Miranda warning, 5, 6, 74, 76, 77, 83, 84, 85, 89, 90, 91, 92, 93, 94, 95, 98
Missouri v. Seibert, 94
Moore, Alvin, 40, 42, 44, 52
"Mutt and Jeff" strategy, 72

N

National Commission on Law Observance and Enforcement, see Wickersham Commission
National District Attorneys' Association, 84
Nedrud, Duane, 84
Nelson, Gary, 58, 60, 61, 70, 71
Newsweek, 89
"Nightline," 86
Nixon, Richard, 92
North Carolina v. Butler, 93

O

Office of Legal Policy, 85
oral argument, 68, 70

P

pauper's form, 65, 66
police brutality, 17, 18, 21, 23, 24, 27, 29, 54, 71, 87
polygraph test, 9
Powell v. Alabama, 18, 19, 20, 21, 22, 33, 34, 47, 48
precedent, 20, 34, 46, 67, 94, 98
pro bono, 44, 66

Q

Queen of Peace Catholic School, 35

R

Rehnquist, William, 94

S

Schmerber v. California, 96
"Scottsboro Nine" case, see
    Powell v. Alabama
self-incrimination, 14, 15, 16, 23,
    29, 44, 45, 68, 74, 95, 96
Shields, Henry, 21, 22
Sixth Amendment, 15, 16, 17,
    23, 25, 27, 32, 40, 45, 46, 47,
    48, 56, 68, 87
Star Chamber, 15
State Boys' School, see Arizona
    State Industrial School for Boys
state laws, 16
Stewart, Raymond, 21
Stewart, Roy Allen, 64, 65, 67
Stewart v. California, 65
Supreme Court of the United
    States, see United States
    Supreme Court

T

testimony, 50, 71, 79, 80, 91
Thompkins, Van Chester, 94, 95
torture, 13, 22
"totality of the circumstances"
    test, see voluntariness test

Tucker case, see *Michigan
    v. Tucker*

U

United States Supreme Court, 6,
    7, 12, 17, 18, 19, 20, 21, 22, 23,
    24, 25, 27, 29, 32, 33, 34, 35,
    40, 41, 42, 43, 44, 45, 49, 57,
    58, 60, 61, 63, 64, 65, 66, 67,
    68, 72, 73, 74, 76, 77, 78, 80,
    83, 90, 91, 92, 93, 94, 96, 97
United States v. Garibay, 93
University of Arizona, 44, 58
University of Wisconsin, 44

V

Vignera, Michael, 64, 65, 67
Vignera v. New York, 65
voluntariness test, 23, 24, 25

W

warning card, 76, 81, 82
Warren, Earl, 33, 71, 74, 92
Warren Court, 33
Westover, Carl Calvin, 64, 65, 67
Westover v. United States, 65
Wickersham Commission, 17
Wickersham Report, 17, 18, 23, 72

Y

Yale Law School, 44
Young, Wilfred, 37, 41, 48, 50, 51
Younger, Evelle, 87, 89